INTERNATIONAL LAW OF
THE RESOURCES OF THE SEA

INTERNATIONAL LAW OF THE RESOURCES OF THE SEA

Reprinted edition with
Supplements

by

SHIGERU ODA

*Judge of the International Court of Justice
former Professor of International Law
Tôhoku University, Japan
Membre de l'Institut de Droit International*

SIJTHOFF & NOORDHOFF   1979
Alphen aan den Rijn, The Netherlands
Germantown, Maryland   USA

ISBN 90 286 0399 9

Revised edition of "International Law of the Resources of the Sea", published
in Volume 127 (1969-II) of the Collected Courses, The Hague Academy of
International Law.

PREFACE

Nearly ten years have passed since the author lectured to the Hague Academy of International Law in 1969 on the subject of the title of this book. In the past decade the international law of the resources of the sea has changed greatly. Last spring the Hague Academy of International Law gave him an opportunity to deliver a number of lectures on this subject at an external programme held in Tokyo. The occasion necessitated a reconsideration of his previous lectures in the light of the changes that have taken place in the last ten years. However, he did not find it necessary to change his basic position on the international law of the resources of the sea and now deems it proper to re-express those original thoughts (printed in Volume II, 1969, of the *Recueil des cours* of the Hague Academy), which, although expressed ten years ago, are still relevant in leading to an understanding of the past developments of the international law of the sea. In this respect his other publications in this area, particularly *The Law of the Sea in Our Time – I: New Developments 1966–1975,* Sijthoff, and "The Ocean: Law and Politics", *Netherlands International Law Review,* Volume 25, No. 2 (1978), should be consulted.

Because the author's present function precludes discussion of delicate issues, and limitations of time have meant little additional material, no alterations have been made, apart from a few minor printing corrections, to the original text but a supplement has been added to each chapter, reflecting additional thoughts, some of which have been previously expressed by the author in other publications. For this reason, the new regime of deep sea mining is not examined. The Introduction, "The United Nations and Ocean Exploration", and Part III, "International Law Relating to Scientific Research and Investigation of the Ocean and Submerged Areas", in the original text, have been omitted because it is felt that in the light of present circumstances their retention in the revised edition is not justified. Though this booklet is not as comprehensive or as up-dated as he would like, the author hopes that this modest work will register his views on the subject among studies of the law of the sea, particularly of earlier days.

The author would like to express his gratitude to his colleague, Judge Roberto Ago of the International Court of Justice, President of the Curatorium of the Hague Academy of International Law, for granting him permission to publish his previous lecture delivered at the Hague Academy in this form.

February 1979   *Shigeru Oda*

OTHER PUBLICATIONS BY THE AUTHOR RELATING TO THE LAW OF THE SEA IN EUROPEAN LANGUAGES

I. Monographs

International Control of Sea Resources, 1962, 215 pp., Sijthoff (Leyden).
International Law of the Resources of the Sea (Recueil des cours de l'Académie de droit international, 1969-II), pp. 353-484.
The Law of the Sea in Our Time - I: New Developments 1966-1975, 1977, 269 pp. (Sijthoff Publications on Ocean Development, Vol. 3).
The Law of the Sea in Our Time - II: The United Nations Seabed Committee 1968-1973, 1977, 332 pp. (Sijthoff Publications on Ocean Development, Vol. 4).

II. Articles

The Territorial Sea and Natural Resources, *International and Comparative Law Quarterly,* Vol. 4, 1955, pp. 415-425.
The Hydrogen Bomb Tests and International Law, *Die Friedenswarte,* Bd. 53, 1956, pp. 126-135.
New Trends in the Régime of the Sea, *Zeitschrift für Ausländisches Öffentliches Recht und Völkerrecht,* Bd. 18, 1957, pp. 61-102, 261-286.
A Reconsideration of the Continental Shelf Doctrine, *Tulane Law Review,* Vol. 32, 1957, pp. 21-36.
El Convenio de Ginebra sobre la Plataforma Continental, *Revista Española de Derecho Internacional,* Vol. 12, 1959, pp. 67-84.
The 1958 Geneva Convention on the Fisheries: Its Immaturities, *Die Friedenswarte,* Bd. 55, 1960, pp. 317-339.
The Concept of the Contiguous Zone, *International and Comparative Law Quarterly,* Vol. 11, 1962, pp. 131-153.
The Extent of the Territorial Sea - Some Analysis of the Geneva Conferences and Recent Developments, *Japanese Annual of International Law,* Vol. 6, 1962, pp. 7-38.
Recent Problems of International High Seas Fisheries: Allocation of Fisheries Resources, *Philippine International Law Journal,* Vol. 1, 1963, pp. 510-519.
Japan and International Conventions Relating to North Pacific Fisheries, *Washington Law Review,* Vol. 43, 1967, pp. 63-75.
Proposals for Revising the Convention on the Continental Shelf, *Columbia Journal of Transnational Law,* Vol. 7, 1968, pp. 1-31.
Boundary of the Continental Shelf, *Japanese Annual of International Law,* Vol. 12, 1968, pp. 264-284.

Possible Future Régime of the Sea-Bed Resources, *Symposium on the International Régime of the Sea-Bed, June 30–July 5, 1969,* pp. 343–362.

International Law of the Sea, 1971, *UN Doc. ESA/RT/Meeting 1/9* (Inter-regional Seminar on the Development of the Mineral Resources of the Continental Shelf, Port of Spain).

The Delimitation of the Continental Shelf in Southeast Asia and the Far East, *Ocean Management,* Vol. 1 (1973), pp. 327–346.

The United Nations Conference on the Law of the Sea – Recent Developments, Present Status and Future Implications, *ECOSOC, Proceedings of the Twelfth Session of the Committee for Co-ordination of Joint Prospecting for Mineral Resources in Asian Offshore Areas, 1975,* pp. 321–338.

The Ocean: Law and Politics, *Netherlands International Law Review,* Vol. 25, 1978, pp. 149–158.

III. Materials

The International Law of the Ocean Development, Vol. I, 1972, 519 pp.; Vol. II, 1974, 579 pp.; loose-leaf service, 1978 Sijthoff (Leyden).

TABLE OF CONTENTS

Preface   v

Other publications by the author   vii

Part I
International law relating to living marine resources . . .   1

Chapter I. *Coastal fishery jurisdiction*   3

1. Presumptive understanding of the concept of the fishery
   jurisdiction   3
2. Extent of the territorial sea   5
   (a) Past practices   5
   (b) Pre-World War II efforts to codify the law on the ex-
         tent of the territorial sea   6
   (c) Claims to extension of seaward jurisdiction in the post-
         war period   6
   (d) Preparations by the International Law Commission for
         establishing a uniform limit of the territorial sea . .   7
   (e) The 1958 Geneva Conference on the law of the sea .   8
   (f) The 1960 Geneva Conference on the law of the sea .   10
   (g) Present law on the extent of the territorial sea . . .   11
   (h) National interests and the extent of the territorial sea .   14
3. Concept of the fishery zone   17
   (a) Fishery zone as proposed at the Geneva Conferences .   17
   (b) The unilaterally-established 12-mile fishery zone . .   17
   (c) Legal status of the unilaterally-established 12-mile
         fishery zone   20
   (d) Reactions of other States to these claims   22
   (e) Mutual recognition of the right to establish the 12-mile
         fishery zone   24
   (f) Evaluation of the 12-mile fishery zone   27

Supplements

1. New efforts by the United States for a 12-mile territorial
   sea in the late 1960s 32
2. Growing support for the 200-mile economic zone . . . 34
3. New concept of the exclusive economic zone 36
4. Certain difficulties in the concept of the exclusive economic zone 39

Chapter II. *Control of the high-seas fishery resources* . . . 41

1. Conservation of fishery resources 41
   (a) Scientific investigation 41
   (b) Control over fishing 43
   (c) Some regional fisheries conventions 45
2. Distribution of the catch of fishery resources 46
   (a) General concepts of distribution 46
   (b) Some examples of arbitrary distribution 48
   (c) The problems in general 54
3. Geneva Convention on high-seas fisheries 60
   (a) Duty of conservation 61
   (b) Special interests of the coastal State 62
   (c) Compulsory settlement of disputes 63

Supplements

1. Aftermath of the Geneva Convention on High Seas Fisheries and the present position of some fishery treaties . . 64
2. High seas fisheries under the Informal Composite Negotiating Text 65

Chapter III. *Special treatment of sedentary fisheries* 69

(a) The problems in general 69
(b) Problems of the king crab 71
(c) Recommendations 74

Supplement 75

Part II
International law relating to marine mineral resources . . .   77

Chapter IV. *Regime of the continental shelf*   79

1. The Continental Shelf Convention   79
2. Fundamental regime of the continental shelf   83
   (a) Drafting of the relevant provisions of the convention   83
   (b) The North Sea Continental Shelf cases   84
3. Outer edge of the continental shelf   85
   (a) Drafting of the relevant provisions of the convention   85
   (b) Interpretation of the provisions   88
4. Boundaries of the continental shelf   89
   (a) Relevant provisions of the convention   89
   (b) Equidistance line   90
   (c) Existence of islands   96
5. Exploitation of the continental shelf and other legitimate
   uses of the superjacent high seas   98
6. Legal status of the superjacent waters of the continental
   shelf   99
   (a) Relevant provisions of the convention   99
   (b) Inevitable exercise of coastal authorities   100
   (c) Installations and their surrounding safety zones . .   101

Supplements
1. Boundaries of the continental shelf   104
2. Parallelism between the exclusive economic zone and the
   continental shelf   106

Chapter V. *Regime of the deep ocean floor*   109

1. Historical backgrounds   109
   (a) Progress of work in the United Nations   109
   (b) Two distinct areas for two different objectives . . .   110
2. Areas beyond the continental shelf   111
   (a) Diverse proposals for outer limit of the continental
   shelf   111
   (b) Policy considerations on the extent of the continental
   shelf   114

3. Regime of the deep ocean floor 115
   (a) Use of this area for the benefit of mankind 115
   (b) Who is entitled to exploit the resources of the deep
      ocean floor? 116
   (c) Problems of sharing profits derived from exploitation:
      interests of developing nations 119
4. Use of the deep ocean floor and the freedom of the high
   seas 122

Supplements
1. United States interests in a wider continental shelf . . 124
2. Deliberations on the extent of the continental shelf at
   United Nations meetings 126
3. A new concept of the continental shelf 128

Index 130

PART I

INTERNATIONAL LAW RELATING TO LIVING MARINE RESOURCES

Three main problems present themselves in connection with international law relating to living marine resources: (1) the coastal jurisdiction which each coastal State exercises to control fisheries off its coast; (2) problems of high-seas fisheries beyond national jurisdictions; and (3) a special problem relating to sedentary fisheries.

CHAPTER I

COASTAL FISHERY JURISDICTION

1. Presumptive Understanding of the Concept of the Fishery Jurisdiction

The first problem is a traditional one, and it deals with how far a coastal State is entitled to control its off-shore fisheries and the kind of competence the coastal State is allowed, under international law, to exercise in that area.

Claims to possession of wider areas of the sea were not unknown in the Middle Ages.[1] Late in the 15th century, Spain and Portugal claimed control over the Western part of the Atlantic Ocean and over the eastern part of the Atlantic and Indian Oceans, respectively, on the basis of a sanction (or "Papal Bull") granted by Pope Alexander VI. Besides Spain and Portugal, Great Britain, which later became a strong advocate of the freedom of the seas, had also once claimed the vast ocean as her own possession.

It was the famous Dutch commentator, Hugo Grotius, who, as counsel to the East India Company, opposed the Portuguese claim that the Indian Ocean should be closed to trade by foreign vessels and attempted to justify the freedom of the sea. He presented his argument in the treatise *"Mare Liberum"*, which was published anonymously in 1609.[2] The opposition which *"Mare Liberum"* aroused was led by Selden of Great Britain. In his *"Mare Clausum"* (1635), Selden analysed past practices and concluded that the private possession of the sea had theretofore been a widely recognised fact of life.[3] Referring to a host of historical facts and precedents, he sought

---

1. See Fulton, T. W., *The Sovereignty of the Sea*, Edinburgh and London, 1911, Introduction.
2. Grotius, H., *The Freedom of the Seas, or the Right Which Belongs to the Dutch to Take Part in the Eastern Indian Trade* (translated by Magoffin, 1916), Carnegie Endowment for International Peace.
3. Selden, J., *The Right and Dominion of the Sea* (translated by James Howell, 1668).

to prove that Great Britain possessed the seas surrounding the British Isles.

At first impression, Grotius' *"Mare Liberum"* and Selden's *"Mare Clausum"* appear completely contradictory in their content. In fact, however, Selden did not deal with the open oceans; while the freedom of the sea which Grotius advocated did not pertain to the sea areas close to land. The claim to the possession of seas near the coast has become the basis of the present regime of the territorial sea. On the other hand, the concept of freedom of the seas has provided the foundations of the regime of the high seas Thus, it can be seen that the division of the ocean into the high seas and the territorial seas has a most respectable historical base.

It is not necessary to discuss in detail the various concepts relating to the territorial sea and the high seas. It is clear that, under the present regime of international law, the sea is divided into these two areas and in each case different rules and regulations obtain. As for the exploitation of sea resources, there is no question that the coastal State is empowered to regulate any such exploitation within its territorial sea and fully to apply its domestic legislation to any person engaged in such activities. Similarly, the coastal State is free to prohibit exploitation by foreigners and thus to monopolise all these resources for itself. On the high seas, however, no State is allowed, at least in principle, to impose its jurisdiction upon any foreign vessels, since the exploitation of sea resources on the high seas falls under the general regime of the high seas.

The existence of these two disparate regimes, namely exploitation under the full control of the coastal State and exploitation of sea resources free from interference by any country, is a fundamental presumption underlying the exploitation of sea resources. Of course, this presumption may be affected in various ways by special international law. The purpose of this presentation will be to determine and to analyse how such changes take place with respect to the various categories of exploitation of sea resources.

2. Extent of the Territorial Sea

If the extent of the territorial seas *prima facie* coincides with the monopoly of marine resources by the coastal State, it is of great importance to determine how far the territorial sea should extend from the coast. This has been one of the most hotly debated subjects in international law.

(a) Past Practices [4]

The concept of a three-mile territorial sea has had a profound influence on the history of international law. While there is no theoretical or normative ground for choosing precisely three miles as a limit of the territorial sea, it may be stated categorically that the major maritime nations have adhered to the three-mile rule. The United Kingdom and the United States have employed the rule and for many years have considered it basic maritime policy. The statements of delegates to the Conference for Codification of International Law convened by the League of Nations in 1930 indicated that 18 of the 36 countries represented were in favour of the three-mile rule.[5] Almost all major maritime countries, including, of course, the United Kingdom and the United States, supported this rule. It is important to note that the States which approved the rule at the 1930 Conference owned 80 per cent. of the world's tonnage.[6]

For the past few centuries, the Scandinavian countries have advocated a four-mile limit. Although no other State had explicitly either admitted or objected to this Scandinavian claim, it seems to have won approval finally with the International Court of Justice decision in 1951 on the Anglo-Norwegian Fisheries dispute.[7] One of the most important members of the dissenting group, the USSR, had

---

4. See, especially, Crocker, H. G., *The Extent of the Marginal Sea*, Washington, 1919; Jessup, P. C., *Law of Territorial Waters and Maritime Jurisdiction*, New York, 1927; Meyer, C. B. V., *The Extent of Jurisdiction in Coastal Waters*, Leyden, 1937.
5. See the table regarding the territorial sea in Hackworth, G. H., *Digest of International Law*, Vol. 1, 1940, p. 628.
6. Statement of the delegate of Great Britain. League of Nations, *Acts of the Codification Conference*, Vol. III, p. 123.
7. I.C.J., *Fisheries Case* (United Kingdom *v.* Norway), Vol. I, pp. 214-586; Vol. III, pp. 9-758.

claimed a 12-mile limit since the time of Imperial Russia more than half a century ago. This claim, taken over by the Soviet Union, was embodied in 1927 in the first comprehensive statute on territorial jurisdiction which established a 12-mile limit.[8]

(b) Pre-World War II Efforts to Codify the Law on the Extent of the Territorial Sea

Late in the last century and early in this, several unsuccessful attempts were made to establish uniform limits for the territorial sea. In successive sessions of such non-governmental institutions as the Institut de Droit International, the International Law Association, etc., the thinking on the extent of the territorial sea was marked by vacillation between a three-mile limit and a six-mile limit.

In 1930 the League of Nations called a conference of plenipotentiary delegates to discuss the codification of certain aspects of international law. The problem of the territorial seas was one of the three topics selected for codification. Despite elaborate preparation for codification of the regime of the territorial seas undertaken by scholars throughout the world, and contrary to the general expectation, this Conference for Codification failed to reach any agreement on the extent which a coastal State is competent to exercise its territorial jurisdiction.[9] Although the Conference passed a resolution recommending a new conference on this subject, the problem remained unsolved at the time of the outbreak of hostilities in 1939.

(c) Claims to Extension of Seaward Jurisdiction in the Post-War Period

The absence of a uniform limit to the territorial sea has made it difficult to give precise legal evaluation to the claims of various States to coastal waters. In the post-war period, a great number of States were inclined to extend their jurisdictional areas beyond the line

---

8. See Reinkemeyer, H. A., *Die Sowjetische Zwölfmeilenzone in der Ostsee und die Freiheit des Meres*, Köln, 1955, 175 pp.; Hartingh, F. de, *Les Conceptions Soviétiques du Droit de la Mer*, Paris, 1960, 193 pp.; Butler, W. E., *The Law of Soviet Territorial Waters*, New York, 1967, 192 pp.

9. League of Nations, *Acts of the Conference for the Codification of International Law*, Vols. I and III.

traditionally drawn as the extent of the territorial sea.[10] The form of those claims has varied greatly. Sometimes the extent of the territorial sea has been simply extended by unilateral proclamations or municipal legislation. On the other hand, certain States have claimed rights exclusively for the purpose of fishing, without touching on the extent of their territorial seas. Some countries, while confining their territorial seas to a narrow belt, have claimed sovereignty over the high seas to a greater extent. Many unilateral claims differ chiefly in point of distance and terminology, but they are still fundamentally similar in so far as they were made with a view to conferring upon each claiming State the right to exercise its jurisdiction over foreign nationals engaged in fishing in the area beyond the traditionally drawn territorial limit. In other words, all of these countries insisted upon their right to subordinate to their own jurisdiction foreign fishermen found in the claimed areas.

The claims of some Latin American countries, especially, should be noted. Chile, Ecuador, and Peru unilaterally legislated a 200-mile maritime zone. They also joined in the Santiago Declaration of 1952, with Costa Rica later subscribing in 1955, which proclaimed sovereignty and jurisdiction of these nations over the sea adjacent to their respective coasts, up to a minimum distance of 200 miles, with the single concession that innocent passage would not be restricted. It is no exaggeration to state that claims of jurisdiction have been asserted, in effect, mainly with a view to securing a national advantage which is best served by exclusive control of the sea's resources. Any ideas which might have been advanced of conservation of fishery resources merely cloaked the true intent of the claims, namely the attainment of an exclusive monopoly for the coastal State.

(d) Preparations by the International Law Commission for Establishing a Uniform Limit of the Territorial Sea

Under such circumstances, the International Law Commission which had been established by the United Nations to undertake the

---

10. See, especially, *UN Legislative Series, Laws and Regulations on the Regime of the High Seas,* Vol. I, 1951; *Laws and Regulations on the Regime of the Territorial Sea,* 1956; *Supplement to the Publication Entitled Laws and Regulations on the Regime of the Territorial Sea,* 1960.

progressive development of international law and its codification, took up the regime of the territorial sea as a priority item on its agenda.

Professor François of the Netherlands served as special rapporteur on this subject; and the process of preparation, discussion, drafting and soliciting comments of governments was repeated. By 1956 several articles on the territorial sea had been adopted by the International Law Commission as a part of its 73 draft articles on the law of the sea.

The International Law Commission was unable, however, to advance any concrete proposals on the extent of the territorial sea. Instead, it presented the following text: [11]

1. The International Law Commission resognizes that international practice is not uniform as regards the delimitation of the territorial sea.
2. The International Law Commission considers that international law does not permit an extension of the territorial sea beyond twelve miles.
3. The International Law Commission, without taking any decision as to the breadth of the territorial sea up to that limit, notes, on the one hand, that many States have fixed a breadth greater than three miles and, on the other hand, that many States do not recognize such a breadth when that of their own territorial sea is less.
4. The International Law Commission considers that the breadth of the territorial sea should be fixed by an international conference.

(e) The 1958 Geneva Conference on the Law of the Sea [12]

In February 1958 a conference on the law of the sea was convened by the United Nations in Geneva to implement the draft articles on the law of the sea as prepared by the International Law Commission (General Assembly Resolution 1105 (XI): 21 February 1957). No fewer than 86 countries sent delegates to this Conference.

The outcome of the Conference was that all proposals regarding the extent of the territorial sea were rejected, and the Convention on the Territorial Sea and the Contiguous Zone was silent on the subject. From the very beginning of the Conference there was little doubt that all the countries of the Soviet and Arab blocs, as well as most Asian, African and Latin American States, would favour the 12-mile limit.

---

11. *Report of the International Law Commission, 1956,* p. 4, art. 3.
12. UN Conference on the Law of the Sea, 1958, Geneva, *Official Records,* Vols. II and III.

They did not accept the proposition that there was any such fundamental rule as a three-mile limit, either in practice or in theory. It was their view that the claim to 12 miles would not change any existing fundamental rule but would only restate the inherent rights of each country. On the other hand, the delegates of the maritime States took the position that the three-mile rule was the only basic principle under international law, and they expressed their wishes, in the respective general debates at the Conference, that the three-mile rule be adopted by the Conference. It appeared clear to all, however, in the light of strong demands made by many newly established States for a wider extent of the territorial sea, that the three-mile rule would be defeated at the Conference. The maritime States themselves had to admit that the Conference, based as it was upon majority rule, could achieve no measure of success unless they were prepared to make certain concessions.

And when some of the maritime States expressed their willingness to accept a six-mile limit, there was no chance for approval of the three-mile limit. The traditional three-mile limit was not even put to a vote. The United Kingdom, which had for centuries been considered a leading proponent of freedom of the seas and of the three-mile rule, indicated, though reluctantly, her readiness to concede a six-mile limit under certain conditions. The Swedish proposal in support of a simple six-mile limit secured the support of only 16 nations. But, on the other hand, the 12-mile proposal advanced by the socialist States and the developing nations failed of adoption because of the objections raised by the advanced maritime countries.

Various compromises were proposed to conciliate between the two extremes of three-mile and 12-mile advocates. Canada tendered a proposal of a six-mile territorial sea with six additional miles as a fishery zone. On the other hand, the United States suggested that continuance of fishing by foreign vessels should not only be allowed but guaranteed within the outer six-mile fishery zone suggested by Canada. But the Canadian proposal gained greater support among the developing countries. Although many maritime States conceded that they could expect no more favourable solution than the United States proposal, neither of the compromise proposals succeeded in securing the necessary majority.

9

(f) The 1960 Geneva Conference on the Law of the Sea [13]

The feeling of the conferees was that the lessening of international tensions and the preservation of peace and order on the seas would be extremely difficult without agreement on the extent of the territorial sea. Therefore, the General Assembly by resolution passed in 1958 called for a second international conference on the law of the sea for the purpose of further considering the problem (General Assembly Resolution 1307 (XIII): 10 December 1958).

At the 1960 Conference on the Law of the Sea, neither the three-mile limit nor the simple six-mile limit was given serious consideration. The maritime States were compelled to make a further concession in limiting to ten years the period during which fishing by foreign vessels would be permitted in the outer six-mile zone beyond the six-mile territorial sea.

The only alternatives before the 1960 Conference were the simple 12-mile territorial sea and the six-mile territorial sea plus a six-mile fishery zone where the fishing rights of foreign States would be phased out within some limited period of time. The maritime States naturally favoured the latter position, but they had to make a still further concession to the effect that a coastal State might be given preferential rights in fishing even beyond the 12-mile limit off its coast. The vote on this proposal ran 54 in favour, 28 against, and 5 abstentions. Had but one of the opposing countries abstained from the voting, this proposal would have been adopted by the two-thirds majority. If the proposal had obtained approval, the law would then have provided for a six-mile territorial sea and a zone beyond of six miles for fishery rights of the coastal State, with the further provision that the fishing rights of foreign States would be phased out within a certain limited period and preferential fishing rights even beyond the 12-mile belt would be granted to the coastal State. The proposal for a flat 12-mile limit advanced by the developing countries and the socialist nations was also rejected. And again, no substantive agreement was reached upon this important subject.

---

13. Second UN Conference on the Law of the Sea, 1960, Geneva, *Official Records*.

(g) Present Law on the Extent of the Territorial Sea

It is difficult to explicate the existing rules of international law on the extent of the territorial sea: even the United Nations Conference on the Law of the Sea on two occasions has failed to reach agreement on the subject. The maritime States were adamant at both Conferences that the three-mile rule was a basic principle of international law and that, if any other rule were to be formulated, it could be done only in a spirit of compromise. In fact, certain of the delegates to the 1958 Conference emphasised that any departure from the three-mile limit was proposed only in a spirit of compromise and that the three-mile limit would be maintained if the Conference failed to agree on an alternative. Although the United Kingdom delegate indicated his readiness to depart from the three-mile limit, he stated that his own proposal of a six-mile limit did not involve the abandonment by his government of the view that the three-mile limit principle still constituted a fundamental rule of law in the absence of any applicable convention to the contrary.[14] The French delegate also noted that, if the compromise changing the three-mile rule were to be rejected, no significance could be attached to the fact that, in the course of the Conference, certain States had proposed that the extent of the territorial sea be fixed at six miles.[15] After all the voting at the 1960 Conference was over, the delegates of Belgium, Greece, Italy, Spain and Portugal indicated that, as the compromise put forward had not obtained the required majority, they did not consider themselves further bound by the vote they had cast.[16]

The United States view, as set forth in the official documents of the Conference, succinctly related the policy of the maritime nations:

Three miles was the sole breadth of territorial sea on which there had ever been anything like common agreement, and was a time-tested principle which offered the greatest opportunity to all nations without exception. Unilateral acts by States claiming a greater breadth of territorial sea were not sanctioned by international law, and conflicted with the universally accepted principle of freedom of the seas. In his Government's view there is no obligation on the part of the States adhering to the three-mile rule to recognize claims of other States to a greater breadth.[17]

14. *UN Conference on the Law of the Sea, 1958*, Vol. III, p. 105.
15. *Id.*, p. 171.
16. *Second UN Conference on the Law of the Sea, 1960*, pp. 32-35.
17. *Id.*, p. 34.

TABLE 3. BREADTH

		3 miles		4 miles		5 miles		6 miles	
Asia	23	China (Rep. of), Japan, Jordan, Malaysia	4			Cambodia *1		Ceylon, Israel, Singapore, Turkey *	4
Oceania	2	Australia,* New Zealand *	2						
Africa	27	Congo (Brazzaville), Congo (Kinshasa), Gambia, Kenya, Liberia, Morocco *	6					Ivory Coast,* Somalia, South Africa (Rep. of),* Tunisia *	4
Western Europe	16	Belgium, Denmark,* France,* Germany, Ireland,* Malta, Netherlands, UK *	8	Finland, Iceland,* Norway,* Sweden	4			Greece, Italy, Portugal,* Spain *	4
Eastern Europe	7	Poland	1						
North America	2	Canada,* US *	2						
Latin America	20	Cuba, Guyana, Nicaragua,* Trinidad-Tobago	4					Colombia,* Dominica,* Haiti, Uruguay *	4
97		27 (10)		4 (2)		1 (1)		16 (9)	

(Asterisk indicates States claiming fishery zones; Figure in parentheses indicates the number of such States.)

On the other hand, the countries of the Soviet bloc, the Afro-Asian group, and Latin America took the failure of the two Geneva Conferences as proof of the complete rejection of the three-mile rule.

The difficulty of talking about a uniform international rule on the extent of the territorial sea thus has remained unchanged.

Available data (see table 3) show that out of a total of 97, 27 countries, including the United Kingdom, the United States, France, the Netherlands, Canada and Japan, maintain the three-mile limit, while 37 nations, including the USSR and a large group of Afro-Asian countries, claim the 12-mile limit for their territorial sea. No

12

TERRITORIAL SEA (as of 1 August 1969)

9 miles	10 miles	12 miles		Others	
		Burma, Cyprus, India,* Iran, Iraq, Kuwait, Pakistan, Saudi Arabia, Syria, Thailand, Vietnam, Yemen	12	Indonesia (archipelago), Philippines	2
		Algeria, Dahomey, Ethiopia, Gabon, Ghana, Libya, Madagascar, Mauritania, Nigeria, Senegal,* Sierra Leone, Sudan, Tanzania, Togo, UAR	15	Cameroon (18), Guinea (130)	2
	Yugoslavia 1	Albania, Bulgaria, Romania, Ukrainian SSR, USSR	5		
Mexico * 1		Brazil, Guatemala, Honduras, Jamaica, Venezuela *	5	Argentina, Chile, Ecuador, El Salvador, Panama, Peru	6
1 (1)	1	37 (3)		10	

country in Western Europe, North America and Oceania claims more than six miles.

Bearing in mind that a simple statistic does not indicate any normative rule concerning the limit of the territorial sea, one may find from this table that it would be extremely difficult to draw any valid conclusions on the existing rules of territorial limits. It seems that the view expressed by the International Law Commission at its last stage of deliberations in 1956 still stands.

As difficult as it is to point to any rule of law in this area as definitive, it is equally hard to suggest any *lex ferenda* regarding the

13

extent of this maritime belt. But at least it may be categorically stated that the extension of the maritime limit is advanced only for the exclusive use of the off-shore areas of each coastal State and in detriment to the community interest as a whole.

(h) National Interests and the Extent of the Territorial Sea

It is pertinent in this respect to examine the factors which create problems in determining the extent of the territorial sea.[18]

(i) Guarantee of Free Navigation

First, those maritime States which maintain large merchant fleets understandably oppose any extension of the territorial sea, since freedom of navigation is assured only on the high seas. But since the right of innocent passage is granted to foreign vessels on the territorial sea, the passage of merchant vessels is of little relevance to the width of this stretch of water. Although the right of innocent passage of merchant ships through the territorial sea is not precisely comparable to free passage on the high seas, it is hardly likely that the distinction between the two concepts can have a bearing on the final determination of the extent of the territorial sea.

(ii) Security Considerations

Security considerations are sometimes raised in support of a completely opposite policy on the extent of the territorial sea. And, indeed, there seem to be valid grounds for claiming a broader territorial sea as a means of maintaining the security of the coastal State. It is no secret that certain developing States are apprehensive about the foreign warships which approach their off-shore areas, and new States have displayed considerable irritation, but from a somewhat different point of view, over the manoeuvres of foreign fleets conducted off their coasts.

The real concern of the United States was clearly outlined by Arthur Dean, President of the United States delegation in both 1958 and 1960, in articles which he published after the first Geneva Con-

---

18. This presentation was made by the author in Oda, S., "The Extent of the Territorial Sea — Some Analysis of the Geneva Conferences and Recent Developments", *Japanese Annual of International Law*, Vol. 6, 1962, pp. 7-38.

ference. First, he was quite frank about the danger of Russian submarines equipped with missiles. He stated:

... if the territorial sea were extended to 12 miles, an enemy submarine (particularly a nuclear submarine which could operate silently for long periods without surfacing) would be able to move about undetected in a neutral State's territorial sea, whereas our surface ships would not operate there without violating the State's neutrality.[19]

Secondly, he found it unacceptable that the territorial sea might be so extended as to limit the manoeuvres of the United States fleet. His statement on 20 January 1960 before the United States Senate Committee on Foreign Relations clearly reflects this position:

Our Navy would like to see as narrow a territorial sea as possible in order to preserve the maximum possibility of deployment, transit, and maneuverability on and over the high seas, free from the jurisdictional control of individual States.[20]

The United States is not likely to give up her rights of sailing her naval fleets in these areas, especially in the Mediterranean Sea and some waters in Asia, and it is probable that some disputes will arise concerning the passage of warships in the zone between six and 12 miles from the coast.

(iii) Fishery Interests

As already indicated there was, in the course of discussions at the 1958 and 1960 Geneva Conferences, an attempt to compromise on a narrower territorial sea by treating fishery interests independently of the regime of the territorial sea.

Many of the delegates considered these interests of overriding importance in the delimitation of the territorial sea. In order to secure a greater advantage in this respect, a large number of States favoured a wider extension of the territorial sea which would serve to exclude foreign fishing from the coastal areas. Those States boasting advanced skills in fishing, however, were very much concerned with the right to fish in off-shore areas of *other* States. Certain statements made at

---

19. Dean, A. H., "Freedom of the Seas", *Foreign Affairs,* Vol. 37, 1958, pp. 83, 90.
20. *US Department of State Bulletin,* Vol. 42, 1960, pp. 251, 259.

the Geneva Conferences by delegates of advanced fishing States clearly indicated that any extension of the territorial sea would represent an intolerable blow to their fishery interests. "Fishery interests" was used to support both a wider and a narrower territorial sea.

The United States was placed in a somewhat delicate position, since, for reasons of security, it could not accept the concept of a broader territorial sea. On the other hand, the United States could hardly oppose the principle of a narrower belt, since a less extensive territorial sea would work to the advantage of American interests fishing off certain Latin American coasts. On balance, however, the United States, throughout both Conferences, seemed prepared to sacrifice fishery interests for coastal security, provided the developing nations would indicate their readiness to accept as the general extent of the territorial sea the narrower belt proposed by the United States chiefly for security reasons.

Thus, the United States might have found itself aligned with the developing nations (a majority of the world), had the more restricted theory of the territorial sea been accepted. On the other hand, the developing States, which regarded fishery interests as the principal benefit of the concept of a territorial sea, would have secured their own interests sufficiently with the injection of a "coastal fishery zone" idea, and this would permit them to leave the limits of the territorial sea as they were. It is significant to note that the developing States conceived the 12-mile fishery zone only in combination with the concept of a narrower territorial sea. The United States would have favoured the 12-mile fishery zone *only if* the narrow limit of the territorial sea had been accepted.

In 1958 the United States proposed that while the territorial sea would be limited to six miles, a coastal State might establish a 12-mile fishery zone, provided that any State whose vessels had fished regularly there for the preceding five-year period would have the right to continue this fishing so long as it observed the conservation regulations of the coastal State. In 1960, as a concession, the United States proposal was amended to limit continuation of fishing by foreign vessels to a period of ten years. While neither of these United States proposals secured the necessary majority at the 1958 and 1960

Conferences, it is important to note that the concept of the fishery zone has been vigorously advocated since the Geneva Conferences.

3. Concept of the Fishery Zone

(a) Fishery Zone as Proposed at the Geneva Conferences

The concept of the fishery zone proposed at the Geneva Conferences may be summarised as follows: First, the 12-mile fishery zone would be a jurisdictional area of the coastal State, which could exercise its powers in the zone, so far as fishing is concerned, in exactly the same manner as within the territorial sea. Although the coastal State would be obliged to permit foreign fishing to continue within its fishery zone, there is no doubt that such fishing would remain subject to the jurisdiction of the coastal State.

Second, in order for foreign fishing to be permitted, a history of past fishing activity was considered a prerequisite. The period of ten years, later five years, was proposed as such a prerequisite.

Third, while it was suggested in 1958 that traditional foreign fishing would be continued for an indefinite period, the idea of a phasing-out of this right was introduced in 1960. Foreign fishing, which would be completely terminated after ten years, would be permitted during that period only as a transitory or interim measure. After this ten-year period, the 12-mile fishery zone would have the same status as the territorial sea, in so far as fishing is concerned.

(b) The Unilaterally Established 12-Mile Fishery Zone

The proposals made by the United States in 1960 for the unilateral establishment of a 12-mile fishery zone find ample support and precedent. Over 20 nations have claimed such a zone while holding to a lesser territorial sea. Among them (as can be seen from tables 4 and 5) are Australia, Canada, Denmark, France, New Zealand, Norway, the United Kingdom and the United States. Brief reference to some of these claims should prove useful.

With the enactment in 1964 of its Territorial Sea and Fishing Zones Act, Canada established a nine-mile fishery zone beyond its three-mile territorial sea. In this outer zone, the laws of Canada in respect of fishing apply in the same way and to the same extent as

TABLE 4.   UNILATERAL ESTABLISHMENT OF THE 12-MILE
FISHERY ZONE (as of 1 August 1969)

Iceland	30 June 1958	effective 1 September 1958
Albania	1 March 1960	
Senegal	21 June 1961	
Mauritania	20 January 1962	superseded by a later claim to 12-mile territorial sea
Morocco	30 June 1962	
Tunisia	26 July 1962	
Uruguay	21 February 1963	
Denmark	20 May 1963	off the coast of Greenland
	26 May 1965	
Rep. of South Africa	29 June 1963	
Turkey	15 May 1964	effective 25 August 1964
Canada	16 July 1964	effective 23 July 1964
U.K.	31 July 1964	effective 30 September 1964
Ireland	1964	
New Zealand	10 September 1965	effective 1 January 1966
Pakistan	19 February 1966	superseded by a later claim to 12-mile territorial sea
Norway	11 June 1966	
Portugal	22 August 1966	
U.S.	14 October 1966	
Brazil	18 November 1966	
Mexico	9 December 1966	
Spain	8 April 1967	effective 2 May 1967
France	7 June 1967	
Australia	8 November 1967	effective 30 January 1968

they do to the territorial sea of Canada. In conformity with this law, which made negotiations on the subject considerably easier, certain States, such as France, the United Kingdom, and the United States, etc., have been authorised to continue fishing in this Canadian zone.[21]

In the same year, the United Kingdom took a similar step by enacting the Fishery Limits Act, whereby the United Kingdom extended its fishery limits to 12 miles from the coast, dividing this area into the six-mile exclusive fishery zone and a six-mile outer belt. Even in the latter zone, domestic law obtains. Foreign fishing vessels are not allowed to enter this zone, unless they fly the flag of States which are parties to a convention concerning the continuation of

---

21. *International Legal Materials,* Vol. 3, 1964, p. 922. See Gottlieb, A. E., "The Canadian Contribution to the Concept of a Fishing Zone in International Law", *Canadian Yearbook of International Law,* Vol. 2, 1964, p. 55; Morin, J. Y., "La Zone de Pêche Exclusive du Canada", *Id.,* p. 77.

TABLE 5. UNILATERAL ESTABLISHMENT OF FISHERY ZONE (as of 1 August 1969)

	6 miles	12 miles	15 miles	18 miles	100 miles	200 miles
Asia |5	Lebanon, Maldive |2	Cambodia, Turkey |2			India |1	
Oceania |2		New Zealand, Australia |2				
Africa 5		Morocco, Tunisia, Ivory Coast, Rep. of South Africa |4		Senegal |1		
W. Europe |8		Iceland, UK, France, Ireland, Denmark, Norway, Spain, Portugal |8				
E. Europe |1		Albania |1				
North America|2		US, Canada |2				
Latin America |7		Colombia, Uruguay, Mexico, Dominica |4	Venezuela |1			Nicaragua, Costa Rica |2
30	2	23	1	1	1	2

fishing in this area. And even this fishing is subject to the United Kingdom rules and regulations on fishing and fishing areas.[22]

In 1966 the President of the United States signed an Act to establish a contiguous fishery zone beyond the territorial sea of the United States. In the outer nine-mile fishery zone beyond her three-mile territorial sea, the United States would exercise the same exclusive rights in respect of fisheries in the zone as it held in its territorial sea, subject to the continuation of such traditional fishing by foreign States within this zone as might be recognised by the United States.[23]

Inherent in these legislative enactments of Canada, the United Kingdom and the United States is the recognition of the right of foreign vessels to continue fishing in the 12-mile zones where a history of such fishing existed.

On the other hand, certain legislation provides simply for a 12-mile fishery zone and recognises no right to the continuation of fishing by foreign vessels. For instance, under New Zealand's Territorial Sea and Fishing Zone Act of 1965, the fishery zone is extended nine miles beyond the three-mile territorial sea. But by providing for the application of the same laws on fishing as obtain in the territorial sea, this Act completely excludes foreign fishing from these areas.[24] There are still further variations on the theme which an examination of relevant laws, country by country, would reveal.

(c) Legal Status of the Unilaterally-Established 12-Mile Fishery Zone

Aside from the question of the continuation of foreign fishing, the legal status of the unilaterally-established 12-mile fishery zone may be summed up as follows:

First, it must be specifically noted that the States regard the 12-mile fishery zone as valid not only with regard to any specific States but also with regard to all States.

Second, the 12-mile fishery zone is an area of fisheries regulation,

---

22. *International Legal Materials,* Vol. 3, 1964, p. 1067.
23. *Id.,* Vol. 5, 1966, p. 1103.
24. *Id.,* p. 1.

where the coastal State may exercise its own jurisdiction in the same manner as in its territorial sea.

Third, the fishery zones of certain States are areas where the fishing is reserved exclusively for the respective coastal State, although continuation of foreign fishing may be recognised in some cases. And even where the continuation of foreign fishing is permitted, such a right is given only to those States which had engaged in fishing in the area in the past. Furthermore, such foreign fishing is subject to the jurisdiction of the coastal State. There is, in addition, legislation which clearly provides that the continuation of foreign fishing will be terminated after the expiration of a certain period of time and the area will then be transformed into an exclusive zone of the coastal State. There is still other legislation which does not clearly indicate whether there is to be a phasing-out of foreign fishing. Even here, however, there is no guarantee that a foreign State will always enjoy the right to continue fishing in the fishery zone. Or, put differently, the continuation of traditional foreign fishing is not a *sine qua non* to the establishment of a 12-mile fishery zone but simply a concession given to foreign States under the regime of the 12-mile fishery zone, which alone is a permanent institution.

In any consideration of national practices with respect to the 12-mile fishery zone, changes in attitude of some of the advanced fishing nations cannot be ignored. It is especially important to note that the United States has abandoned her original position on the 12-mile fishery zone. As noted earlier, the United States in 1966 had unilaterally established a 12-mile fishery zone off its own coasts. In commenting on the bill pending before the Congress, the Legal Adviser of the Department of State explained that, in the view of the Department, the fishery zone of nine miles beyond the three-mile territorial sea contravened no rule of international law.[25] Of course, the United States still adheres to a three-mile territorial sea. The 12-mile fishery zone, proposed at the Geneva Conferences by the United States *only* as a means of inducing the developing coastal States to agree to a narrow territorial sea, and acceptable to the United States

---

25. US, *Hearings before the Subcommittee on Merchant Marine and Fisheries of the Senate Committee on Commerce on S. 2218; 18 May 1966.* Serial No. 89-65, p. 20.

(at least in 1958 and 1960) only in conjunction with universal approval of the narrower belt of coastal-State jurisdiction, has now become an independent concept with its own *raison d'être.*

(d) Reactions of Other States to these Claims

The unilateral establishment of a 12-mile fishery zone certainly affects, in a varying degree, other States which have had fishing interests in the claimed areas. The fact is, however, that few States have protested against these unilateral claims. There are even some examples where other interested States which may have been thus affected have acquiesced in the claims by concluding bilateral agreements with the claimant States.

Even before asserting jurisdiction over the 12-mile fishery zone, the United Kingdom had acceded to similar claims made by Denmark and Iceland in 1959 and 1961, respectively.[26] On the other hand, the United Kingdom, which in 1964 unilaterally established a 12-mile fishery zone, succeeded in securing approval of its action from Norway, Poland and the USSR.[27] In most cases of these bilateral agreements, the right to continue to fish in the 12-mile fishery zone of the other party to the agreements is given in return for acquiescence in the unilateral claims to the 12-mile fishery zone. But this right is to be phased out after a certain period of time.

Apparently, there is only one country which still explicitly opposes the unilateral establishment of a 12-mile fishery zone: Japan, which itself has never unilaterally established such a zone. Encountering considerable problems arising from the unilateral establishment of the zone by other States, Japan has sought practical solutions through negotiation.

At the outset of this course of action, Japan negotiated with the United States, which had claimed a 12-mile fishery zone in 1966. A fisheries agreement was concluded in 1967 between Japan and the United States, for fishing by Japanese "in the waters which are contiguous to the territorial sea of the United States and extend to a limit of 12 nautical miles" from the United States coast.[28] The agreement

---

26. *UN Treaty Series*, Vol. 337, p. 416; Vol. 397, p. 275.
27. *Id.*, Vol. 548, p. 63; Vol. 539, p. 153; p. 159.
28. *International Legal Materials*, Vol. 6, 1967, p. 745.

did not specifically refer to the "United States fishery zone". Japanese traditional fishing would still continue in some specified areas within the United States 12-miles waters, but the Government of Japan would take necessary measures to ensure that, with this exception, Japanese fishing vessels would not engage in fishing in these waters. The agreement explicitly states that "nothing in the present arrangement should be deemed to prejudice the claims of either Government in regard to the jurisdiction of a coastal State over fisheries". In other words, fishing by Japanese nationals and vessels in this area is considered by the Government of Japan to be fishing on the high seas and by the United States Government as fishing within its own fishery zone.

Agreements of a similar kind were reached by Japan, with New Zealand in 1967 [29] and with Mexico and Australia in 1968.

Japan's success in achieving practical solutions vis-à-vis its relations with the foregoing nations secures its right to continue fishing within the 12-mile zone of other States for only a limited period of time. It is also entirely possible that during this period these States will not seek to extend their jurisdiction over any Japanese vessels fishing within the 12-mile zone. But, because these States have not relinquished their claims to the 12-mile fishery zone, it is quite likely that they may wish in the future to exercise jurisdiction over Japanese fishing vessels within these areas pursuant to their domestic legislation. This, in their view, would be completely in conformity with the rule of international law.[30] In addition, there will probably be no opportunity, after the various specific periods have ended, for Japan to renew its right to continue fishing in the 12-mile fishery zones of the States involved. In the case of the United States, Japan was allowed fishing for only a two-year period. Although this permission was renewable, and has actually been renewed up to the present time, there is no assurance that the United States will continue to grant this concession indefinitely.

---

29. *Id.*, p. 736.
30. According to the view of the United States State Department, "the United States has *not recognized* any traditional fishing rights of Japan, although the United States has *allowed* Japan to continue fisheries in certain areas of the contiguous zone where Japan has conducted operations in the past" (italics added). 90th Cong., 1st Sess., *House Report* No. 999, p. 182.

(e) Mutual Recognition of the Right to Establish the 12-Mile Fishery Zone

There are, however, examples of international agreements under which the contracting parties recognise the mutual right to establish a 12-mile fishery zone.

(i) UK-Norway Fisheries Agreement of 1960 [31]

In point is the 1960 agreement between the United Kingdom and Norway on fishing off the coast of Norway. The Governments of the United Kingdom and Norway, taking into account the formula presented at the 1960 Geneva Conference with respect to the six-mile territorial sea plus an additional six-mile fishery zone, agreed on the total exclusion of United Kingdom fishing vessels from the Norwegian 12-mile zone after 1970. The continuance of United Kingdom fishing in the outer six-mile zone of Norway up to 1970 would not be objected to by Norway. Pursuant to this agreement, Norway the following year, under its Fishery Zone Act of 1961, established a 12-mile fishery zone.

(ii) European Fisheries Convention of 1964 [32]

The most important example of the mutual recognition of the right to establish a 12-mile fishery zone is the European Fisheries Convention of 1964. An international conference was convened in London between December 1963 and March 1964 at the invitation of the British Government. Delegates from 16 countries in Europe adopted the text of a fisheries convention under which the participating States sought "to define a regime of fisheries of a permanent character". They agreed that each contracting party would recognise the right of any other contracting party to exercise exclusive fishing rights within a belt of six miles from the coast. However, the right

---

31. *UN Treaty Series*, Vol. 398, p. 189.
32. *International Legal Materials*, Vol. 3, 1964, p. 469. See Johnson, D. H. N., "European Fishery Limits", *Developments in the Law of the Sea 1958-1964*, pp. 48-74; De Breucker, J., "La Convention de Londres sur la Pêche du 9 mars 1964", *Revue Belge de Droit International*, 1966, pp. 142-166; Vignes, D., "La Conférence Européenne sur la Pêche et le Droit de la Mer", *Annuaire Français de Droit International*, X, 1964, pp. 670-688.

to fish in the area between six and 12 miles offshore might be exercised by the contracting parties, where fishing vessels had habitually fished there for the preceding ten years, namely between 1 January 1953 and 31 December 1962. The power of the coastal State to regulate the fisheries in the outer belt is to be exercised to prevent discrimination, in form or in fact, against fishing vessels of other contracting parties engaged in fishing pursuant to the provisions of the Convention.

Following execution of the European Fisheries Convention, some of the parties, notably the United Kingdom (1964), Denmark (1966), Portugal (1966), France (1967) and Spain (1967), enacted domestic legislation on the 12-mile fishery zone.

(iii) Japan-Republic of Korea Fisheries Agreement of 1965 [33]

The Fisheries Agreement of 1965 between Japan and the Republic of Korea is also of interest. Japan, which had never theretofore recognised unilateral claims to a 12-mile fishery zone, entered into an agreement with the Republic of Korea that each would possess the right to establish a 12-mile fishery zone from which the fishing vessels of the other party would be excluded. This agreement lasts for five years.

(iv) Conclusion

It may be concluded, upon analysis of these three conventions, that the parties to these agreements view the 12-mile fishery zone to be established as under the plenary jurisdiction of the coastal State. In other words, the coastal State would have the unrestricted right to exercise its jurisdiction with respect to fisheries in this 12-mile area.[34]

A second problem exists as to whether these fishery zones are valid with regard to the contracting parties only. It is true that in the Japanese view, the 12-mile fishery zone derives solely from the

---

33. *International Legal Materials,* Vol. 4, 1965, p. 1128.
34. See Windley, D. W., "International Practice Regarding Traditional Fishing Privileges of Foreign Fishermen in Zones of Extended Maritime Jurisdiction", *American Journal of International Law,* Vol. 63, 1969, pp. 490-503.

agreement with the Republic of Korea (which expires five years from its inception) and is not to be construed as existing outside the agreement. It is submitted, however, that territorial title is invested with legal significance only when it is claimed in relation to all the States of the world. The Norwegian Fishery Zone Act of 1961, under which that country's 12-mile fishery zone was established, was enacted pursuant to the 1960 Agreement with the United Kingdom, but this Act seems to cover more ground than the implementation of the 1960 Agreement only. It seems also clear that, quite aside from the provisions of the preamble to the European Fisheries Convention which stated a desire to define a fisheries regime of a permanent character, it was the consensus among the contracting parties to this multilateral convention that the establishment of the 12-mile fishery zone would lead to a new regime of the law of the sea. Witness the fact that a number of the contracting parties to this Convention have established a 12-mile fishery zone even vis-à-vis States not signatories to the Convention. For example, the French decree of 1967 was intended to supplement the European Fisheries Convention, but, in point of fact, the French established a 12-mile fishery zone even beyond the waters to which the Convention was applicable.

Under the 1960 Agreement between Norway and the United Kingdom and the 1965 Agreement between Japan and the Republic of Korea, fishing by one party within the other's 12-mile fishery zone would be completely prohibited. The European Fisheries Convention, on the other hand, permits a contracting party whose fishing vessels had fished there in the past, to continue fishing within the outer six-mile belt. The duration of this privilege is nowhere indicated. The Convention is also silent with respect to its own duration, but, after an initial period of 20 years, any contracting party may terminate its obligations under the Convention. Upon such termination, the 12-mile fishery zone itself is not relinquished, but fishing by other States within this zone is terminated. It thus seems quite safe to state that the 12-mile fishery zone has been established as a permanent regime, and it will be possible for the concession granted to foreign fishing to be terminated after this 20-year period.

(f) Evaluation of the 12-Mile Fishery Zone

To sum up: the proposals presented at the 1958 and 1960 Geneva Conferences, chiefly by the United States, make up one important aspect of the regime relating to the 12-mile fishery zone. Another facet of the problem reflects itself in the practice of certain States of establishing unilaterally the 12-mile fishery zone and the reaction of other States to this practice. And, third, there exists a body of international agreements which grant to the contracting parties certain fishing rights within the 12-mile zone.

On the strength of the foregoing, some conclusions may now be drawn. If the 12-mile fishery zone were accorded the same status as the territorial sea with respect to fishing, there would be, *prima facie*, a conflict with the regime of the high seas, because, as has been noted earlier, fishing by any vessel beyond the limit of the territorial sea should be free from interference by any State except the State of its flag.

It is important to ascertain whether the 12-mile fishery zone, although in concept a clear contradiction of the regime of the high seas, nevertheless presents a *fait accompli* under the present regime of international law. It is sometimes contended that this zone finds justification by analogy to the 12-mile contiguous zone, which is recognised under the Geneva Convention on the Territorial Sea and the Contiguous Zone. This view seems to be untenable.[35] Under the aforementioned Convention, the contiguous zone may be claimed by the coastal State only for customs, fiscal, immigration or sanitation purposes. This exercise of jurisdiction is permissible only because it does not substantially infringe upon any of the legitimate high-seas interests of other States, such as navigation and fishing. By claiming the 12-mile contiguous zone, the coastal State simply intends to protect the legitimate interests which it is entitled to enjoy within its own territorial jurisdiction, but it may not encroach upon freedom of use, such as fishing, by other States. It is not mere coincidence that the 1958 Convention on the Territorial Sea and the Contiguous Zone

---

35. See Oda, S., "The Concept of the Contiguous Zone", *International and Comparative Law Quarterly*, Vol. 11, 1962, pp. 131-153.

27

does not mention fisheries as one of the interests to be reserved to the coastal State under the concept of the contiguous zone. It is the author's contention that the 12-mile fishery zone is fundamentally and intrinsically different from the 12-mile contiguous zone. Even though the contiguous zone may be acceptable as an admissible exception to the regime of the high seas, the same reasoning will not cover the 12-mile fishery zone.

It is therefore necessary to inquire only whether past practice provides sufficient grounds to justify the establishment of a 12-mile fishery zone which, in principle, is at odds with the rule of international law.

A number of proposals submitted in favour of the 12-mile fishery zone at the 1958 and 1960 Conferences received wide support among the delegates, and they may be taken as instrumental in advancing the claim of a 12-mile fishery zone as a customary rule of law.

In addition, the practices of various States must be considered as factors supporting the concept of a 12-mile fishery zone. Table 6 indicates the various claims to jurisdiction over fisheries asserted by States in terms of either "territorial sea" or "fishery zone". Of 100 States listed, 56 have claimed 12-mile fishery jurisdiction, 33 in terms of the territorial sea and 23 in terms of the fishery zone. Those States still confining their fishery jurisdiction to three miles number 17. And if one lumps together claims to four miles, six miles and 10 miles, 29 States still adhere to the principle of fishery jurisdiction over an area extending less than 12 miles from the coast. Not only is this figure significant, but it is also important to note that the United States and the United Kingdom, which might have been strongly affected by the exclusion of their fishing from the areas off the coasts of other States, have moved to support the principle of 12-mile fishery jurisdiction. Yet, while the United States could have advocated the 12-mile fishery zone only if the concept of a narrower territorial sea were accepted, that nation is now inclined towards recognising a 12-mile fishery zone without reference to a narrower territorial sea.

And, finally, the general recognition of the right to establish a 12-mile fishery zone through multilateral or bilateral conventions may be viewed as meaning that such a zone has validity not only for the signatory State but for all other nations as well. If we count these

TABLE 6. EXTENT OF FISHERY JURISDICTION (As of 1 August 1969)

	Total		Asia	Oceania	Africa	W. Europe	E. Europe	North America	Latin America
3 miles	17	T. 17	4	0	5	4	1	0	3
		F. 0	0	0	0	0	0	0	0
4 miles	2	T. 2	0	0	0	2	0	0	0
		F. 0	0	0	0	0	0	0	0
6 miles	9	T. 7	3	0	1	2	0	0	1
		F. 2	2	0	0	0	0	0	0
10 miles	1	T. 1	0	0	0	0	1	0	0
		F. 0	0	0	0	0	0	0	0
12 miles	56	T. 33	11	0	13	0	5	0	4
		F. 23	2	2	5	8	0	2	4
15 miles	1	T. 1	0	0	1	0	0	0	0
		F. 0	0	0	0	0	0	0	0
18 miles	2	T. 1	0	0	1	0	0	0	0
		F. 1	1	0	0	0	0	0	0
100 miles	1	T. 0	0	0	0	0	0	0	0
		F. 1	0	0	1	0	0	0	0
130 miles	1	T. 1	0	0	0	0	0	0	0
		F. 0	0	0	0	0	0	0	1
200 miles	8	T. 6	0	0	0	0	0	0	6
		F. 2	0	0	0	0	0	0	2
archipelago	2	T. 2	2	0	0	0	0	0	0
		F. 0	0	0	0	0	0	0	0
Total	100	T. 70	20	0	21	8	7	0	14
		F. 30	5	2	6	8	0	2	7

T. = territorial sea   F. = fishery zone

States which are parties to the conventions that recognise, even on a consensual basis, the right to establish a 12-mile fishery zone, the previous statement may be restated to show that, out of 100 States, 62 claim a 12-mile fishery jurisdiction, while only 23 still adhere to the concept of a more circumscribed area.

Although certain claimants have attempted to justify the 12-mile fishery zone by arguing its relation to the conservation of fishery resources, such a zone has nothing to do with the universal interest in conservation. The fishery zone is merely an area over which the coastal State claims jurisdiction for the purpose of monopolising sea resources found therein, thus to deprive other States of the opportunity of engaging in fishing. There appears to be no reasonable ground for suggesting the 12-mile zone for exclusive fishing by the respective coastal State. But one cannot ignore recent developments. If for no other reason than to preserve the stability of the international community, that is to say, to maintain the balance between exclusive interests of the various coastal States and the community interest as a whole, acceptance may be suggested of the idea that each coastal State has the right to control all fishery resources within its 12-mile off-shore areas. However, unless there is to be a gradual extension of fishery limits which will lead to a division of the entire ocean among the various coastal States, claims by these States in derogation of high-seas interests should be clearly delimited.

It is suggested that as soon as possible the United Nations endeavour to generalise the concept of the 12-mile fishery zone. Delay may have serious repercussions, since the claims of certain coastal States are year by year becoming more far-reaching. What may satisfy a majority this year may be unacceptable to the majority the next year. Past experience at the 1958 and 1960 Geneva Conferences has brought us this lesson.

In order to halt an endless expansion of the respective claims by various coastal States to fishery jurisdiction, the immediate convocation of a world-wide convention on the 12-mile fishery zone seems mandated. Any State should be free, of course, to grant fishing concessions within this area to any foreign national, since, in principle, each coastal State should be entitled to exclusive fisheries rights within the 12-mile areas off its own shores.

Many of the developing States remember clearly that, at the 1960 Conference, it was the United States which suggested certain further preferential fishing rights beyond the 12-mile fishery zone for the benefit of the coastal State involved and that this suggestion received wide support even among the countries of the Western group. The idea of preferential fishing rights for the coastal State is, however, ambiguous and subject to a variety of interpretations. At a later stage this problem will be discussed in greater detail in connection with high-seas fisheries.

SUPPLEMENT TO CHAPTER I

1. New Efforts by the United States for a 12-Mile
Territorial Sea in the late 1960s

The American idea of trading the 12-mile fishery zone for a narrower territorial sea did not bear fruit in the Geneva Conferences on the Law of the Sea in 1958 and 1960. But the determination of the United States to maintain a narrower territorial sea limit for security and military considerations remained unchanged, and the quest was continued in order to discover some way to forestall the general movement towards 12-mile territorial sea. However, it became apparent in the latter half of the 1960s that it was already impossible to reverse the trend towards the extension of the territorial sea and persuade the developing nations to withdraw their unilateral legislation establishing a 12-mile territorial limit. How then could the substance of a narrower territorial sea be obtained? Finding it advisable to secure the free navigation of warships and military aircraft within the 12-mile breadth of the coast in certain critical areas, the United States began sounding out the views of some NATO countries, the Soviet Union and others in 1968 and 1969. The United Nations Seabed Committee had already started its work when the rumour of the United States initiative began spreading around the world.

In 1970, the United States, for the first time, publicly began airing its views. On 2 February 1970, in his report to the Congress on *United States Foreign Policy for the 1970s,* President Nixon stated that the most pressing issue regarding the law of the sea was the need to achieve agreement on the breadth of the territorial sea in order to head off the threat of escalating national claims over the oceans.[1] That evening, in his statement at Philadelphia, John R. Stevenson, the Legal Advisor to the State Department, disclosed the future policy of the United States concerning the territorial sea.[2] This policy, based on the 12-mile territorial sea, stipulated, however, that all vessels and aircraft, including military ones, should be given freedom of passage through straits used for international navigation. With this announcement, the United States began its campaign to fix the limit of the territorial sea at 12 miles. While recognizing the 12-mile territorial sea, the objective of the United States was to secure free navigation for warships and military aircraft in certain specific parts of this area. In order to achieve this objective, some compensation would have to be

---

1. *US Department of State Bulletin*, Vol. 62, No. 1602 (9 March 1970), pp. 273, 314.
2. *US Department of State Bulletin*, Vol. 62, No. 1603 (16 March 1970), p. 339.

offered to the developing nations. Ten years before, when the 6-mile territorial sea was at issue, it was the recognition of a 12-mile fishery zone, and in 1970 it had to be something more. As compensation for the burden to be imposed upon the coastal State, in connection with the free transit of ships and of warships and military aircraft, the United States attempted to offer the concept of preferential fishing rights beyond the 12-mile territorial sea to some developing nations whose murmurings were increasing in strength.

In the summer session of 1971 the United States presented to the Seabed Committee its idea in the form of three articles.[3] Article 1 simply mentions the 12-mile territorial sea, Article 2 states that in straits used for international navigation, all ships and aircraft in transit should enjoy the same freedom of navigation and overflight as if on the high seas. Article 3 may be summarized as follows: in the event that an appropriate international or regional organization is unable or unnecessary to regulate the high seas fisheries, a coastal State may adopt unilateral measures of conservation and allocation of the fisheries in any area of the high seas adjacent to its territorial sea, and the percentage of the allowable catch that can be harvested by that State shall be preferentially allocated to it annually. With regard to enforcement of fisheries regulations, however, actions taken by the coastal State are limited to inspection and arrest of vessels, and only the State of nationality of the offending vessel has jurisdiction to try any case or impose any penalties regarding the violation of fishery regulations. The 12-mile territorial sea itself was no longer at issue. The idea of freedom of transit for all vessels and aircraft, including warships and military aircraft, irritated some countries bordering on straits. Preferential fishing rights of coastal States were offered at the expense of existing fishing rights of major distant-water fishing nations, in order to gain freedom of passage for warships and military aircraft through certain straits. The United States' attempts appeared to lure the largest catch with the smallest bait.

The position taken by the developing countries had not changed greatly since the 1958 Conference on the Law of the Sea. For them, the 12-mile territorial sea had been a premise, and not something to be granted or given as a compensation. If this was the case, the American claim to free passage through straits as if they were high seas naturally appeared to them as a violation of their sovereignty. Furthermore, fishing interests beyond the 12-mile territorial sea had been considered by the developing nations to be an acquired right, but, again, not something to be granted as compensation. They simply wished to institutionalize the regime of a fishery zone which would extend as far from the coast as possible. They were confident that their wishes would eventually be realized. Thus, they were not willing to wait for the somewhat ambiguous preferential fishing rights to be granted under the American draft.

---

3. UN Doc. A/AC.138/SC.II/L.4.

2. Growing Support for the 200-Mile Economic Zone

From the point of view of the developing nations, it seemed clear that the recognition of the 12-mile territorial sea was but an endorsement of what had already been a customary rule of law and, therefore, its recognition should be unconditional. Moreover, they considered the resources found in their adjacent seas as belonging inherently to them and not as something that could be bargained for, i.e., in return for recognition of the right of free transit through straits. It is against this background that the concept of the economic zone came into being.

The economic zone concept was introduced in a clearly defined form for the first time by the representative of Kenya at the annual meeting of the Asian-African Legal Consultative Committee held at Lagos, Nigeria, in January 1972.[4] A width of 200 miles from the coastline was explicitly mentioned in this regard. It soon became apparent that the proposal could command wide support from many of the developing nations of Africa and Asia, for whom (at least for the time being) substantial economic interests could be expected only from the resources in their adjacent waters. This concept was subsequently confirmed at the African States Regional Seminar on the Law of the Sea held at Yaoundé, Cameroon, in June 1972.[5] The meeting of Ministers of the Caribbean countries held in June 1972 at Santo Domingo also endorsed similar principles by declaring a "patrimonial sea" of 200 miles.[6] These two ideas seemed to contain in common the feature that the coastal States would be permitted to establish an extensive jurisdictional zone outside the territorial sea (not to exceed 12 miles), in which they would have exclusive enjoyment of all resources, both living and non-living.

With overwhelming support from the developing nations, Kenya proceeded formally to submit the 200-mile economic zone proposal to the Seabed Committee in the summer of 1972.[7] While the freedom of navigation was still to be guaranteed, all resources, either fishery or mineral, in or under the ocean, would be placed under the jurisdiction of the coastal States. This proposal was considered by many of the developing nations of Africa and Asia as a way to realize what they regarded as their special and legitimate interests. The Latin American countries, which had claimed a 200-mile maritime sovereignty for the past twenty years, naturally gave their strong support. Even among developed States, a number were likely to take the position that coastal States should have a certain jurisdiction with respect to the utilization, conservation and management of the living resources of the sea in areas adjacent to their coasts. Canada spoke of delegating powers to conserve and manage fishery resources to coastal States as custodians of the

---

4. Asian-African Legal Consultative Committee, *Report of the Thirteenth Session*, held in Lagos, 1972, p. 155.
5. See UN Doc. A/AC.138/79.
6. See UN Doc. A/AC.138/80.
7. UN Doc. A/AC.138/SC.II/L.10.

34

international community. In the summer of 1972, Australia and New Zealand submitted a working paper, recognizing exclusive jurisdiction of the coastal State over the living resources of the superjacent waters of the continental shelf.[8] It was for the coastal State under this proposal to determine the allowable catch of any particular species and to allocate to itself that portion of the allowable catch, up to 100 per cent., that it could harvest. However, where the coastal State was unable to take 100 per cent. of the allowable catch of a species, it had to allow the entry of foreign fishing vessels with a view to maintaining the maximum possible food supply. Being unable to remain indifferent to such a development, the United States seemed to be prepared to make any necessary concession, if the freedom of transit through straits could be guaranteed and began to negotiate a compromise along the lines of the economic zone as far as the resources aspect was concerned, and thought it fit to amend its original fishery proposal.

By the 1973 summer session, a flood of proposals concerning the 200-mile zone had been introduced. In principle, two separate ideas were seen in these proposals as far as the nature of the zone was concerned. One school of thought was represented by the Latin American group which claimed categorical control over this zone. While limiting the territorial sea to 12 miles, a proposal submitted by Colombia, Mexico and Venezuela suggested that the coastal State might establish a 200-mile patrimonial sea.[9] In addition, under this proposal, the coastal State would have a special interest in maintaining the productivity of the living resources in an area adjacent to the patrimonial sea. The proposal of Uruguay provided that every State would be entitled to determine the breadth of its territorial sea within 200 miles[10] and the Brazilian proposal also prescribed that each State had the right to establish the breadth of its territorial sea within reasonable limits, not exceeding 200 miles, taking into account geographical, social, economic, ecological and national security factors.[11] The proposal of Argentina suggested that there should be, apart from the 12-mile "territorial sea", an area of sea up to a distance of 200 miles or up to a greater distance coincident with the epi-continental sea.[12] A coastal State would have "sovereign rights" over this area which meant the volume of water covering the seabed at an average depth of 200 metres, which might be further than 200 miles from its coast. In this area, a coastal State would have "sovereign rights" over the natural resources.

Parallel with these moves made by the Latin American nations, the sponsoring nations of the Kenyan concept of the 200-mile exclusive economic zone were growing in number, particularly in Africa and Asia. In 1973 fourteen African nations, including Kenya, submitted draft arti-

---

8. UN Doc. A/AC.138/SC.II/L.11.
9. UN Doc. A/AC.138/SC.II/L.21.
10. UN Doc. A/AC.138/SC.II/L.24.
11. UN Doc. A/AC.138/SC.II/L.25.
12. UN Doc. A/AC.138/SC.II/L.37.

cles along the same lines as suggested by Kenya the previous year.[13] In draft articles on fisheries by Canada, India, Kenya and Sri Lanka it was specifically provided that the coastal State might allow nationals of other States to fish in its exclusive economic zone, subject to such terms, conditions and regulations as it might prescribe.[14] But the jurisdiction and control over all fishing activities within the zone would lie with the coastal State and any difference or dispute concerning the limits of the zone, and the interpretation or validity of the terms, conditions or regulations for fishing, would be settled by the coastal State.

Once the 200-mile exclusive economic zone is institutionalized, one-half of the world's oceans will be incorporated in this regime, thus dividing the globe into three parts: land, economic zones and the high seas. The concept of the 200-mile exclusive economic zone, or the broad coastal zone, had some difficulties in finding support among land-locked and other geographically disadvantaged States which would be unable to benefit from it. Two African land-locked States, Uganda and Zambia, proposed regional or sub-regional economic zones where fishing could be reserved for all the States within the region: they also proposed that relevant regional authorities should have the exclusive right of mineral exploitation on behalf of all States in the region.[15] Six land-locked or geographically disadvantaged States, Afghanistan, Austria, Belgium, Bolivia, Nepal and Singapore, suggested that coastal States should have the right to explore and exploit all living and non-living resources in an X-mile zone, where the neighbouring land-locked and coastal States have the right to participate in fishing on an equal and non-discriminatory basis.[16]

3. New Concept of the Exclusive Economic Zone

Despite the fact that many nations supported the 200-mile zone, both in the United Nations Seabed Committee and the Law of the Sea Conference in the first part of the 1970s, there were not many examples of the unilateral establishment of 200-mile zones in that period. It was only a few years ago that a number of countries started establishing unilateral 200-mile zones: the United States and the Soviet Union in 1976 and Canada and the countries of the European Communities in 1977.[17] Even Japan, which had registered strong disapproval of a widely extended jurisdiction for any coastal State, claimed a 200-mile fishery zone for herself in 1977.[18] Naturally the contents of these unilateral claims or laws are not the same. Some try to cover all the economic

---

13. UN Doc. A/AC.138/SC.II/L.40.
14. UN Doc. A/AC.138/SC.II/L.38.
15. UN Doc. A/AC.138/SC.II/L.41.
16. UN Doc. A/AC.138/SC.II/L.39.
17. *International Legal Materials,* Vol. 15 (1976), pp. 634, 1381, 1372, 1425.
18. *Japanese Annual of International Law,* Vol. 21 (1977).

activities in the zone, while others are limited simply to fishing activities. In addition it must be noted that during the past few years several countries have also claimed a 200-mile zone as their own territorial sea.

The trend towards the 200-mile zone is now irresistible and in the light of the deliberations at the Law of the Sea Conference there does not remain any problem in having a uniform limit of 200 miles for economic zones. A question which still remains to be solved is related to the legal nature of this 200-mile zone and to what kind of competence the coastal State will be entitled to exercise in this zone. If the ocean is to be considered, in accordance with the traditional dualistic concept, as consisting of the high seas on the one hand and the territorial sea on the other, this problem might have been more important. In fact, discussions have been held at various conferences, particularly in 1976, as to whether the exclusive economic zone would still be a part of the high seas or belong to the category of the territorial sea. This problem had already arisen: it had to be dealt with when the 12-mile fishery zone became institutionalized in international law. However, this presumption of dualism is not of absolute importance and there is no reason why a third regime should not be created, separate from both the territorial sea and the high seas, and it seems quite clear that this zone is able to claim that its status is *sui generis*.

In the Informal Composite Negotiating Text of 1977,[19] Part V, consisting of 21 articles, covers the exclusive economic zone. The exclusive economic zone is defined in the Text as "an area beyond and adjacent to the territorial sea, subject to the specific legal regime established in this Part, under which the rights and jurisdictions of the coastal State and the rights and freedoms of other States are governed by the relevant provisions of the present Convention" (Article 55). To explain it in a more detailed way, "the coastal State has ... sovereign rights for the purpose of exploring and exploiting, conserving and managing the natural resources, whether living or non-living, of the seabed and subsoil and the superjacent waters, and with regard to other activities for the economic exploitation and exploration of the zone, such as the production of energy from the water, currents and winds ... [and] jurisdiction ... with regard to ... the establishment and use of artificial islands, installations and structures; ... marine scientific research; [and] the preservation of the marine environment ..." (Article 56-1 (*a*), (*b*)). On the other hand "all States, whether coastal or land-locked, enjoy ... the freedoms ... of navigation and overflight and of the laying of submarine cables and pipelines, and other internationally lawful uses of the sea related to these freedoms such as those associated with the operation of ships, aircraft and submarine cables and pipelines ..." (Article 58-1). In other words, in the 200-mile exclusive economic zone the coastal State may exercise sovereign rights with respect to some

---

19. UN Doc. A/CONF.62/WP.10 and Add. 1.

limited purposes while other States can continue to enjoy some other rights which they could have enjoyed on the high seas. As far as the exploitation of natural resources, either living or mineral, are concerned, the coastal State will have jurisdiction over all such activities, whether carried out by its own nationals or by foreigners. The coastal State will apply its legislation governing these activities to all and sundry, and any person charged with a violation of this legislation will undoubtedly be tried by its courts and punished, if found guilty. The mode of exercise of jurisdiction by the coastal States within the economic zone is no different from that exercised by them within their own territorial sea, and as far as the development of the natural resources of the sea is concerned, the competence to be exercised by the coastal States within their economic zone is equivalent to that exercised in the territorial sea. Yet, quite differently from the territorial sea, the coastal State will have to assume in its exclusive economic zone some responsibility for the conservation and utilization of fishery resources. "The coastal State shall determine the allowable catch of the living resources in its exclusive economic zone" and "shall ensure through proper conservation and management measures that the maintenance of the living resources in the exclusive economic zone is not endangered by over-exploitation" (Article 61-1, 2). The responsibilities imposed upon the coastal State as regards conservation make the exclusive economic zone different from the territorial sea, where the coastal State does not assume any such responsibility under international law.

The most original idea of the 200-mile exclusive economic zone is derived from the introduction of the principle of optimum utilization of fishery resources. The Informal Composite Negotiating Text suggests: while the coastal State shall determine its capacity to harvest the living resources of its exclusive economic zone, "it shall, through agreements or other arrangements and pursuant to the terms, conditions and regulations, ... give other States access to the surplus of the allowable catch", where it "does not have the capacity to harvest the entire allowable catch" (Article 62-1, 2). In the case of the 12-mile fishery zone, foreign fishing might continue in the zone, but only upon the basis of treaties agreed upon with the coastal State or as a consequence of concessions granted by the coastal State. It was suggested in 1958 and 1960, for instance, that traditional foreign fishing should be guaranteed in the fishery zone, but still this was to be phased out sooner or later. But, in the case of the 200-mile exclusive economic zone, foreign fishing will be guaranteed for the surplus of the allowable catch of the coastal State.

In addition, the interests of land-locked States and geographically handicapped nations will also be taken into account, as without the support of these countries, the 200-mile economic zone could hardly have been institutionalized. Article 69 states: "Land-locked States shall have the right to participate, on an equitable basis, in the exploitation of an appropriate part of the surplus of the living resources of the exclusive economic zones of coastal States of the same subregion or region, taking

38

into account the relevant economic and geographical circumstances of all the States concerned ... The terms and conditions of such participation shall ... be determined by the States concerned through bilateral, sub-regional or regional agreements. ... Developed States shall be entitled to participate in the exploitation of living resources only in the exclusive economic zones of developed coastal States of the same sub-region or region." Similar provision is made in Article 70 applicable to States with special geographical characteristics, in other words, geographically handicapped nations.

Thus the competence of the coastal State within its exclusive economic zone will have to be placed under certain international restrictions: firstly, the exploitation of the surplus by other nations, and secondly, the participation in harvesting by some geographically handicapped nations. These features of an international nature of the 200-mile exclusive economic zone appear to make this zone *sui generis* and therefore quite distinct from the territorial sea and the high seas.

4. Certain Difficulties in the Concept of the Exclusive Economic Zone

The author would like to refrain from making any value judgment, either positive or negative, on this new institution of the law of the sea. However, he cannot but make a few comments from a purely legal point of view. It seems that the practical application of these principles of international nature of the 200-mile economic zone will not be as simple as envisaged in the Informal Composite Negotiating Text.

With regard to the surplus of the allowable catch which cannot be harvested by a coastal State, that State will be obliged to give other States access to it. We must note that the coastal State never has to harvest the catch in its exclusive economic zone only through its own nationals and with its own technologies. Even the least-developed country is able to harvest the maximum of the allowable catch by granting concessions to any specific foreign person or corporation with which it is free to enter into negotiations. Various factors, which shall be taken into account in giving access to other States, in case the coastal State does not have the capacity to harvest the entire allowable catch, are enumerated in the Text (Articles 62 and 63). In fact, it will be easy for any least-developed country to avoid this obligation and to invite any specific person or corporation to engage in harvesting the maximum allowable catch determined in terms of conservation in its 200-mile exclusive economic zone. In other words, any person or corporation is free to come to any coastal nation to offer the most profitable return in order to obtain exclusive fishing rights in the 200-mile exclusive economic zone. Thus the principle of access of other nations to the surplus will eventually become meaningless, and the 200-mile exclusive economic zone will eventually be assimilated to the territorial sea, where the coastal State is free to grant any concession, to exploit the sea resources to any person or corporation by its own will, except that some land-locked States with special geographical characteristics will continue to be allowed to participate in the exploitation of the living resources. In giving access to other States the coastal State is required to take into account all relevant factors. In the case of participation of land-locked States and States with special geographical characteristics, the coastal State will again be required to take into account the relevant economic and geographical circumstances of the States concerned. However, no degree or order of priorities for the relevant factors is suggested by the Text.

The second point which might embarrass legal writers in interpreting the provisions relating to the exclusive economic zone is related to the status of land-locked States. It is suggested in the Text that land-locked States shall have the right to participate in harvesting fishery resources of the exclusive economic zone of adjoining coastal States under the terms and conditions to be determined by the States concerned through bilateral, sub-regional or regional agreements. Take just one example: which is the adjoining coastal State in Switzerland's case? Is it France, Germany or Italy, or are all these three countries considered adjoining coastal States which will be obliged to give effect to Switzerland's right to harvest fish in their own exclusive economic zone? It will also be extremely difficult to define a State with "special geographical characteristics". It is also suggested in the Text that the developed land-locked States shall be entitled to exercise their rights only within the exclusive economic zone of adjoining developed coastal States and that developing coastal States which are situated in a sub-region or a region whose geographical peculiarities make such States particularly dependent for the satisfaction of the nutritional needs of their populations upon the exploitation of the living resources in the exclusive economic zone of their neighbouring States, and developing coastal States which can claim no exclusive economic zone of their own, shall have the right to participate, on an equitable basis, in the exploitation of living resources in the exclusive economic zones of other States in a sub-region or region. In defining the right of the State concerned, it may well be asked how a distinction can be made between the developing State and the developed State.

In addition, as has been seen in the forum of the Asian-African Legal Consultative Committee some years ago, the question may also be raised as to why the access of land-locked States to the exploitation should not be extended so as to cover mineral resources.

These are just a few examples, but the provisions of the Text concerning the exclusive economic zone will undoubtedly meet many practical difficulties in its application to concrete cases, though the principle of this regime seems to have secured general approval. Some difficulties will also be faced in cases where neighbouring States, either adjacent or opposite, will have to draw the boundaries of their respective exclusive economic zones among themselves. Mention will be made of these problems in connection with the boundaries of the continental shelf.

CHAPTER II

CONTROL OF HIGH-SEAS FISHERY RESOURCES

The belief that the resources of the sea are inexhaustible, and the
corollary idea that their exploitation should go unregulated, is no
longer supported by the facts. Although there still exist vast untapped
ocean treasuries, some control over the exploitation of these marine
resources is needed if their fullest utilisation is to be assured. Conservation, which is of course a subject that must be discussed in
connection with high-seas fishery resources, is a universally accepted
concept of fishery science. Although all States are now in agreement
on the need for conservation, once demand for fishery resources
exceeds supply, the nations of the world will inevitably clash on the
matter of their respective fair shares of these resources. Thus, it is
essential to take up in detail the problem of allocation of these
resources among the nations. And, in this connection, special
attention must be given to the problem of the increasing demands of
coastal States which seek special advantage for their coastal fisheries
beyond their own fishery jurisdiction. Finally, some comment will be
made on the Convention on the High-Seas Fisheries adopted at the
Geneva Conference on the Law of the Sea in 1958.

1. Conservation of Fishery Resources

An examination of prior practices indicates that two types of
measures have been used to conserve marine resources. The first
involves scientific investigation of fish stocks as a preliminary step
towards effective control of fishing. The second and more important
type of conservation measures involves the actual control of fishing itself with a view towards conserving these resources.

(a) Scientific Investigation

To start with the first type of conservation measures: certain permanent international organisations exist which are concerned mainly

41

with scientific research on the stock of fish in various areas. For example, the International Council for the Exploration of the Sea, formed as early as 1902 and reorganised under a Convention in 1964, has as its purpose the encouragement of and reporting on research and development relating to fishery resources.[1] The Council works principally with the North Atlantic European nations, including the USSR, although the United States and Canada are members of the Council. Another example is the Inter-American Tropical Tuna Commission, which was established under a 1949 Convention to undertake, through its own staff, scientific research on tuna in the Eastern Pacific Ocean.[2] The membership of the Commission, originally consisting of the United States and Costa Rica, has since been increased by the addition of Panama, Ecuador and Mexico. The Commission's staff was charged with the responsibility of providing scientific rationales for maintaining resources and preventing serious overfishing. There have been many other fishery commissions created, mostly since World War II, by various international conventions on fisheries. There are marked differences in the powers and competence with which these commissions are invested. Most of the commissions issue extensive reports which describe the progress made in developing various regulations and the results of the scientific research on which these regulations are based.

In addition, the problem of fisheries falls within the jurisdiction of the FAO, under the sponsorship of which regional fisheries councils, such as the Indo-Pacific Fisheries Council and the General Fisheries Council for the Mediterranean, have been established to deal with oceanographic, biological and technical aspects of the problems of development and proper utilisation of living marine resources.

In 1965, the FAO decided to strengthen its mechanism dealing with fisheries and to establish the Committee on Fisheries as a permanent body under its Council. The stated purpose of the Committee is the study of the problems of international fisheries; and it was this organisation which recommended the establishment of the Indian Ocean Fisheries Commission and the Middle East Atlantic

---

1. *International Legal Materials*, Vol. 7, 1968, p. 302.
2. *UN Treaty Series*, Vol. 80, p. 3.

Commission, sponsors of international co-operation in research on fishery resources.

In the late 1960s, the United Nations has deemed it extremely important to encourage and to bolster scientific research on the fishery resources of the ocean. By Resolution 1381 of 1968 on long-range programmes for the exploration of the sea, the Economic and Social Council urged the General Assembly to endorse the concept of a co-ordinated long-term programme of oceanographic research designed to increase, in the interests of world economic development, the resources available to all the peoples of the world. And in its 1968 Resolution 2414 on international co-operation in problems related to the oceans, the General Assembly endorsed the concept proposed by the Economic and Social Council. Another Resolution 2413 adopted by the General Assembly in 1968 related to exploitation and conservation of living marine resources: governments of member States are invited to increase international co-operation in the field of development and exploitation of living marine resources outside the limits of national jurisdiction, having regard to the special needs and interests of the developing countries.

(b) Control over Fishing

The necessity of joint conservation measures has come to be widely recognised. The Truman Proclamation, promulgated just after the cessation of World War II hostilities, drew particular attention to this need for the first time. On 28 September 1945, President Truman announced that, in view of the pressing need for conservation and protection of fishery resources, the policy of the United States would aim at the establishment of conservation zones in those areas of the high seas contiguous to the coast of the United States wherein fishing activities had been, or, in the future, might be, developed and maintained on a substantial scale.[3] This policy, unilaterally established by the United States, aroused world interest in the conservation of marine resources.

The desirability of maintaining marine resources at their maximum sustainable yield is commonly conceded. No State will categorically

---

3. *American Journal of International Law*, Vol. 40, 1946, Supplement, p. 46.

object to conservation measures, since the goal of conservation is to serve the common interests of all nations.

Conventions established on a regional basis may perhaps be the most feasible means of conserving resources, and a number of such conservation conventions have been concluded.

Three main themes run through the various conventions on fisheries conservation.

First, whatever the mode of expression may be, the maintenance of the maximum sustainable yield of the stock is always the final goal of these conventions. In the post-war conventions especially, this aim is generally set forth in the preamble.

Second, the application of effective conservation measures in terms of regulation of the conduct of fishing operations on the high seas is explicitly provided for in international conventions, since it is a basic principle of international law that all States are free to fish on the high seas unless otherwise bound by specific international agreements. The enforcement of the provisions of the conventions, or of any measures subsequently adopted by international commissions set up under these conventions, falls within the responsibility of each contracting party with respect to the fishing vessels flying its flag. This obligation derives from the general principles governing the high seas, whereunder any vessel on the high seas enjoys immunity, in time of peace, from the control of any power and the authority of States other than its flag-nation.

Third, generally, conservation measures impose their burden equally upon all signatory States. Each nation complies with the same restrictions as to fishing methods, which are made uniformly applicable to all signatory powers for the purposes of conservation. It is the actual differences in the fishing technology or economic power of the various countries and not any legal institutions which dictate the quantities which each nation may catch, for competition in fishing is not denied within the limitations prescribed (on a scientific basis) to promote conservation. The idea of equal access to fisheries and equal limitations on fishing is theoretically fundamental to the conservation programme provided for in each convention. In this field as in many other fields, the underlying rationale of free competition is one of the basic values endorsed by modern history.

(c) Some Regional Fisheries Conventions

A brief sketch of some regional fisheries conventions is in order at this point.

The International Convention for the Northwest Atlantic Fisheries was signed in 1949 in Washington, D.C., and became effective in 1950.[4] The United States, Canada, and a number of European countries, including the USSR, are parties to this Convention. The convention area covers generally the waters off the western coasts of Greenland, and the coasts of Labrador, Newfoundland, Nova Scotia and New England. The International Commission of Northwest Atlantic Fisheries established under the Convention develops programmes and co-ordinates research carried out by member governments. Recommendations to governments on regulations may be made regarding the following measures: (i) establishing open and closed seasons; (ii) closing of spawning areas or areas populated by small or immature fish; (iii) establishing size limits for any species; (iv) designating fishing gear and appliances the use of which is prohibited; (v) prescribing an over-all catch limit for any species of fish.

Since the 1946 Convention for the Regulation of Meshes of Fishing Nets and the Size-Limits of Fish applicable to the area of the North-East Atlantic did not attain its objective, a new North-East Atlantic Fisheries Convention signed in 1959 in London, was entered into to supersede the former Convention.[5] The new Convention, which became effective in 1963, established a North-East Atlantic Fisheries Commission charged with keeping under review fisheries in all waters of the North-East Atlantic and Arctic Oceans; determining which measures may be required for the conservation of fish stocks and the rational exploitation of the fisheries in the area; and making recommendations on such matters as regulation of the size of mesh of fishing nets or the size limits of fish that may be retained, the establishment of closed seasons or closed areas, and the regulation of fishing gear.

The International Convention for the Conservation of Atlantic Tunas, concluded in 1966 at Rio de Janeiro, became effective in

---

4. *UN Treaty Series,* Vol. 157, p. 157.
5. *Id.,* Vol. 486, p. 157.

March 1969 for the United States, Canada, France, Spain, Ghana, the Republic of South Africa and Japan. The International Commission for the Conservation of Atlantic Tunas is responsible for the study of populations of tuna, including research on their abundance, biometry and ecology, the oceanography of their environment, and the effects of natural and human factors upon them in the areas covering all waters of the Atlantic Ocean. The Commission may, on the basis of scientific evidence, make recommendations designed to maintain the populations of tuna in the convention areas at levels which will permit the maximum sustainable catch.

It should be noted that conservation measures vary according to the various international conventions, and the functions of international commissions set up under these conventions are not always the same. Nevertheless, the measures provided for in international conventions or suggested by international commissions fall into the following general categories: limitations on the sizes of fish; closed areas; closed seasons; and limitations on the type of gear. Attention should be directed to the fact that the restrictions through these measures on the conduct of fishing are applicable equally to all the contracting parties of the respective conventions, and, hence, it is the actual difference in the fishing power of each participating nation which results in a differing catch for each nation. And, equally important, violation of any regulation is punishable only by the flag-nation of the vessel guilty of the breach of law.

2. Distribution of the Catch of Fishery Resources

(a) General Concepts of Distribution

There is little doubt that over-fishing will lead to the extinction of fishery resources; and the necessity of conserving fishery resources has never been contested by any nation. Conservation is a basic concept of fishery science, a concept which no State has opposed. However, the principle of free competition among States obtains only where demands upon resources do not overwhelmingly exceed the amount of allowable catch, and conservation measures take the form of restrictions on permissible fishing gear, fishing seasons, or fishing areas. If a fundamental change in circumstances should occur, each

State will undoubtedly be inclined to minimise its own sacrifice and to maximise its own share of resources quite independently of any reasoning in favour of preferential distribution of resources.

This problem may best be illustrated by a simple example: If the total possible catch of a certain species is 150, and prudent conservation practice demands that the total allowable catch be only 100, the burden of abstaining from harvesting the additional 50 will have to be imposed in some way upon the States concerned in exploiting the available 100. Each State may, of course, freely compete in fishing within the total allowable catch of 100. Free competition, however, does not satisfy States which so substantially pre-empt the fisheries concerned that fishing by any newcomer will necessarily decrease their own catch, nor will it be acceptable to nations with less advanced technologies and economies.

In such cases, conflict will inevitably occur between two parties who might otherwise agree upon the desirability of conservation of marine resources. One will adhere to traditional arguments of free competition in fishing on the high seas, especially since its own technology and economy can bring to it a larger share of resources, while the other, seeking to assure itself of a constant, preferably large, share of the resources, might invoke all kinds of reasoning in an attempt to keep its competitors from exploiting the areas it considers most important. The problems inherent in the allocation of limitations have in fact made it difficult, perhaps impossible, to compromise conflicting national interests even among those States which are most vitally concerned with the conservation of resources.[6]

---

6. This problem of allocation and distribution of fishery resources was presented by the author in Oda, S., "New Trends in the Regime of the Seas— A Consideration of the Problems of Conservation and Distribution of Marine Resources", *Zeitschrift für Ausländisches Öffentliches Recht und Völkerrecht,* Bd. 18, 1957, pp. 61-102, 261-286. See Christy, F. T. and Scott, A., *The Common Wealth in Ocean Fisheries,* pp. 175-191; Christy, F. T., "The Distribution of the Sea's Wealth in Fisheries", *The Law of the Sea* (Proceedings of the Second Annual Conference of the Law of the Sea Institute), p. 106.

(b) Some Examples of Arbitrary Distribution

(i) The North Pacific Fisheries Convention of 1952

The North Pacific Fisheries Convention of 1952 is a particularly apt illustration of this point.

The negotiations which produced the 1952 Convention among Canada, Japan and the United States, took place in an atmosphere of anxiety, prior to the signing of the Peace Treaty of Japan. The American fishing industry was apprehensive over the possible return of the Japanese as competitors in Alaskan waters, where certain stocks had already been fully utilised by the Americans and Canadians. One of the most serious problems considered at the tripartite negotiations was whether any of the participating States had acquired any rights or privileges regarding fishing on the high seas.

The United States delegate proposed that any State which had recently begun fishing operations should be required to waive its right under international law to exploit high-seas fisheries with respect to those resources which had been so fully utilised in the past that future intensive fishing would be unwise. Thus, the waiver requirement for purposes of conservation did not apply to all countries but only to newcomer States. Japan, on the other hand, argued the principle of free access and free competition on the high seas, although she did not oppose the implementation of certain conservation efforts. Without reference to the general principle, the United States succeeded in preventing Japan from fishing in certain specified fisheries.[7]

The main proposal emanating from the 1952 Convention is the abstention formula, which requires that pursuant to agreement a State abstain from fishing. This State receives nothing in return, while the other party to the agreement, exempted from the obligation of abstention—for whatever reasons might be considered justifiable—is entitled to maximum utilisation of the resources in the convention area. According to the Convention, Japan agrees to abstain from fishing certain stocks of fish in some parts of the high seas, while Canada and the United States agree to continue to carry out necessary

---

7. *UN Treaty Series,* Vol. 205, p. 65.

conservation measures for those stocks. In effect, the abstention formula ensures a maximum share to one party, while giving nothing in return to the other.

There is general discontent with the 1952 Convention. The United States is not satisfied because it feels that Japanese fishermen are still able to fish for North American salmon on the high seas west of the provisional line drawn at longitude 175° W. Japan, on the other hand, wishes to see the elimination of the abstention formula. Towards the end of the ten-year term of the Convention, in negotiations in 1963 and 1964, Japan voiced disapproval of the abstention formula. In the course of deliberations the Japanese delegate argued that the abstention formula was inherently unfair since it was actually designed for the protection of the fishing industries of certain countries rather than for conservation of fishery resources. The Japanese delegate proposed a new convention which would replace the abstention formula with a provision stating that joint conservation measures should be established on a scientific and non-discriminatory basis, and that fishery management conducted by the United States should be given due consideration in determining these joint conservation measures. The United States rejected this proposal on the theory that the abstention formula provided a clearly defined procedure for dealing with special situations where certain stocks of fish had been made more productive by extraordinary efforts of a particular nation. The United States delegate concluded that the existing convention provided a basis for resolving current North Pacific fishery problems and would promote sound and progressive precedents for the development of international practice in this field.

The negotiations of 1963 and 1964 failed to produce any definitive results, and the 1952 North Pacific Fisheries Convention remains in force.

(ii) The Northwest Pacific Fisheries Convention of 1956 [8]

A further illustration of the problem lies in the Convention for the Northwest Pacific Fisheries, concluded in 1956 between Japan and

---

8. *American Journal of International Law,* Vol. 53, 1959, p. 763.

the USSR. In that year, Japan and the USSR had entered into negotiations to provide for the regulation of high-seas fishing efforts in the Northwest Pacific Ocean. The negotiations took place immediately after the USSR had issued a decree purpoting to regulate salmon fishing in the high-seas areas of the Sea of Okhotsk.

One of the chief features of the Northwest Pacific Fisheries Convention of 1956 is the limitation of annual salmon catch on the high seas. Germanely, salmon spawns in rivers, spends its life in the ocean and then returns to the same river to die. The total allowable catch of the high-seas salmon is determined by the Japan-Soviet Northwest Pacific Fisheries Commission established pursuant to the Convention. The USSR does not engage in salmon fishing on the high seas on a large scale, nor does it contemplate doing so in the future, most Russian salmon fishing taking place in the rivers of the USSR. Consequently, the provisions of the Convention do not significantly affect Russian salmon fishing, while Japanese salmon fishing within the convention area on the high seas is subject to control by the Commission. The domestic policies of the USSR on conservation within her territorial rivers are of vital importance to the Commission in setting forth conservation measures applicable to Japanese fishing vessels on the high seas. This Convention has subordinated an over-all policy of high-seas fishing for migratory salmon to conservation policies unilaterally pursued by the USSR within her own territory. Thus, theoretically, the stocks of salmon in the Northwest Pacific could be distributed in such a way as to be advantageous to the USSR, which has a free hand in adopting fishing policies within her territorial limits.

As a result, the determination of the total annual allowable catch of salmon has been probably the most difficult task facing the Commission at its yearly sessions. The problem proved to be especially vexing during the early years of the Commission's existence. Since 1957 the Commission at its annual meetings has devoted upwards of 100 days to a discussion of this matter. Theoretically, a reduction in quotas affects both nations, but the reality is that only Japan is regulated because the Convention extends solely to international waters. Because salmon are an anadromous fish, the USSR is able to take significant quantities of salmon by operating within its territorial seas.[9] It is thus in principle free to take as much salmon as it wishes inside its own territorial seas.

(iii) Whaling in the Antarctic

Mention should also be made of another interesting example of the allocation of marine resources among the various States.

Antarctic whaling had been open to those countries which, under the 1946 Convention for the Regulation of Whaling, were able freely to compete for their maximum share within the total limit set by the International Whaling Commission.[10] Japan, Norway, the Netherlands, the United Kingdom and the USSR have been engaged in Antarctic whaling since 1957 in expeditions known as the "whaling olympic". These activities have been generally regarded as typical conservation measures on an international level. However, it has become in recent years increasingly difficult to maintain a system of free competition.

In 1957 for the first time an agreement was concluded to set for each of the parties thereto quotas of catches. The signatories represented whaling companies from Japan, the Netherlands, Norway and the United Kingdom. The USSR did not participate and thus maintained a free hand in determining the size of its own whaling effort. A conference of the Antarctic whaling countries recommended in 1958 that 20 per cent. of the permitted Antarctic catch be allocated to the USSR and that discussion on the allocation of the remaining 80 per cent. among Japan, the Netherlands, Norway and the United Kingdom be undertaken with a view to reaching an agreement among the five nations. It further recommended that none of the five countries concerned transfer a factory ship to another country without transferring a corresponding portion of its quota.

The United Kingdom and the Netherlands have withdrawn from the whaling competition in the Antarctic under the decision of the International Whaling Commission handed down at the latest session in June 1969 and only Japan (55 per cent.), Norway (9 per cent.) and the USSR (36 per cent.) participate in the allowable Antarctic whaling

---

9. It would be unfair not to mention that the USSR caught 56,223 tons of salmon in 1966, while Japan caught 111,760 tons in the Northwest Pacific.
10. *UN Treaty Series,* Vol. 161, p. 72.

TABLE 7. CATCH OF ANTARCTIC WHALING (BLUE WHALE UNIT)

	Allowable Catch	Share				
		Japan	Norway	USSR	UK	Netherlands
original		33%	32%	20%	9%	6%
1953/54	16,000				5	6
1954/55	15,500					6
1955/56	„					
1956/57	15,000	(14,500 for this year)				
1957/58	„					
1958/59	„					
1959/60	„					
1960/61	—	(suspension of the catch limitation)				
1961/62	—	(„ „ „ „)				
1962 Arrangements						
1962/63	15,000	41	28	20		
1963/64	10,000	46	28	20		
1964/65	„ (8,000 as voluntary limitation)	52	28	20		
1965/66	4,500	52	28	20		
1966/67	3,500	1,633 BWU (47%)	800 BWU (23%)	1,067 BWU (30%)		
1967/68	3,200	1,493 (47%)	731 (23%)	976 (30%)		
1968/69	„	„	„	„		

52

catch of 2,700 blue-whale units for the year 1969-1970. Free competition by each nation within the limits of the total allowable catch is no longer tenable, at least with respect to Antarctic whaling. (See table 7.)

(iv) Fur Seal Conventions of 1911 and 1957

The Conventions of 1911 and 1957 relating to fur seals in the Pacific present some unique problems in the conservation of living marine resources.[11] (The fur seal is also a migratory animal.) Under these four-party Conventions, Canada, Japan, the United States and the USSR agree to prohibit pelagic sealing on the high seas of the North Pacific Ocean. The Convention provides that, in return for the prohibition of sealing on the high seas, the parties without fur seal rookeries shall be assured certain compensation from the parties possessing such rookeries. Of the total number of sealskins taken commercially each season on the lands of the United States and the USSR, there are to be delivered, at the end of the season, 15 per cent. each of the gross, in number and value thereof, to Canada and Japan (which have no breeding rookeries for fur seals) by both the United States and the USSR, which do have breeding islands. The Conventions contain the unique concept that the absolute prohibition of high-seas exploitation is compensated for by arbitrary distribution of the total land catch, thus assuring the abstaining States of a certain portion of the total yield. This means, in other terms, that a quota system was adopted by these Conventions.

(v) Conclusions

Analysis of the effect of these conventions reveals that certain of the contracting parties have been successful in securing preferential shares (sometimes 100 per cent.) of the admissible total catch in some of the high-seas areas. This is not to prejudge, however, that such a concept of preferential shares to some specific States is reasonable or unreasonable. It should only be pointed out that such a concept of sharing resources through some arbitrary means will be inevitably

---

11. *American Journal of International Law,* Vol. 5, 1911, Supplement, p. 267; *UN Treaty Series,* Vol. 314, p. 105.

brought up, whenever the stock of fishery resources is so extensively exploited that intensive regulation, namely limitation of total catches, is mandated in order properly to preserve fish stock from extinction.

(c) The Problems in General

In connection with the distribution and allocation of marine resources within the allowable total limit established for purposes of conservation, two sets of problems must be faced: those of newcomer States and those of coastal States.

(i) Newcomer States

Certain fundamental questions will certainly be raised in future if States outside any fishery convention claim a share of marine resources which have been exploited to the fullest, where any additional fishing will place impossible burdens on those States which had been engaged in fishing the same areas. But the argument must be made that these newcomer States are at least theoretically entitled to claim a certain share of the resources. This leads us to the question of how to induce newcomer States to stay out of fishing stock which has been exploited to the fullest, or, alternatively, how to introduce a formula of abstention put forward by the United States in its negotiations with Japan in 1951.

The concept of abstention, which was crystallised in the 1952 Convention among Canada, Japan and the United States, has been strongly advocated by the United States on various occasions. At the International Technical Conference on the Conservation of the Living Resources of the Sea, which met in 1955 at Rome, the United States strongly urged this idea.[12] The United States, together with Canada, proposed in its comments on the 1955 draft of the International Law Commission that the abstention formula be included in the final draft convention on the law of the sea then being prepared by the

---

12. Herrington, W. C., "Comments on the Principle of Abstention", *Papers Presented at the International Technical Conference on the Conservation of the Living Resources of the Sea, 1955, Rome* (UN Doc. A/CONF. 10/7), pp. 344, 349.

International Law Commission.[13] At the 1956 session of the International Law Commission, a United States member recommended that the abstention formula be included in the provisions dealing with newcomer States.[14] But several other members of the Commission asserted that the proposal, which dealt with the distribution of catches rather than with the conservation of fish stocks, had no place in a document aimed at the conservation of resources.[15] They warned that the abstention formula was at odds with the over-all spirit of the draft of the Commission and that it might easily lead to situations where a group of States would attempt to exclude nationals of other countries from a particular fishing ground. The International Law Commission decided against including this formula in the draft.

The Geneva Conference of 1958, taking up the problem of conservation, was faced with the very difficult question of allocation of resources.[16] The United States delegate proposed that explicit rules be formulated on the practical mechanics of the abstention formula. The USSR delegate, on the other hand, maintained that this concept was at variance with the principle of equality of rights and the concept of freedom of fishing, and that discrimination should not be practised against newcomers to those fishery grounds already being exploited by other States. He found it difficult also to understand why the principle, which was intended solely to prevent overfishing, would apply only to newcomer States or to those which had not been regularly fishing the stock. The delegates of Japan, Norway, Sweden, the Netherlands, France, Portugal, Bulgaria, Poland, Spain, Germany and the United Kingdom all expressed opposition to the United States proposal on the abstention formula. Confronted with such strong opposition (which included even the Western countries), the United States withdrew its proposal and submitted a modified draft resolution. This draft resolution was ultimately rejected by a vote of 31 in favour and 20 against, with 8 abstentions, the requisite two-thirds majority not being obtained. Thus, the principle of abstention

---

13. *Yearbook of International Law Commission, 1956*, Vol. II, pp. 91, 93; pp. 41, 42.
14. *Id.*, Vol. I, p. 122.
15. *Id.*, pp. 123-125.
16. *UN Conference on the Law of the Sea, 1958*, Vol. V, pp. 102-110.

which the United States had been developing since the 1952 Convention was rejected by the 1958 Geneva Conference.

(ii) Problems of Special Interests of the Coastal State

Another new and very ambiguous concept with respect to the international law of fisheries talks of "special interest" of the coastal State. This principle is not to be confused with the claims, mentioned earlier, by some coastal States to more widely extended fishery jurisdiction. The validity of the concept of a preferential share for coastal States was explored during the course of the 1958 and 1960 Geneva Conferences.

At the 1958 Conference, particularly, the idea of a preferential share for the coastal State in special cases was strongly advanced by the delegate from Iceland, who argued that, where the total yield was insufficient to satisfy the demands of all who wanted to fish in the area, the people of the coastal State should have priority in satisfying their own requirements. Iceland submitted a formal proposal to the Conference to the effect that the coastal State would be entitled to preferential rights in coastal resources, pointing out that a coastal State which depended on coastal fisheries should be permitted to secure for itself as great a share as necessary without having to compete with other States. This proposal found support among many of the Asian and Latin American nations, which would most likely have supported any concept in favour of the interests of the coastal State. The proposal was rejected however, by a vote of 30 in favour to 21 against, with 18 abstentions, with the necessary two-thirds majority not being met.

At the 1960 Conference, the maritime States made certain concessions on recognition of a preferential status for the coastal State in respect of allocation of fisheries in off-shore areas. With the full agreement and advice of the United States, the delegates of Brazil, Cuba and Uruguay submitted a proposal which would permit a coastal State to claim preferential fishing rights in any area of the high seas adjacent to its exclusive fishery zone, when it was scientifically established that special conditions made exploitation of high seas fisheries in that area of fundamental importance to the economic development of the coastal State or to the subsistence of its population.

56

This concession of a preferential status was locked into the proposal that six miles be maintained as the limit of the territorial sea chiefly for the purpose of navigation and security. The proposal of a six-mile territorial sea plus an additional six-mile fishery zone, together with preferential rights beyond the 12-mile limit, however, failed to obtain the requisite two-thirds majority by a single vote, 54 votes being in favour and 28 against. Thus, the Second Geneva Conference (1960) on the Law of Sea ended without producing agreement on a preferential share for coastal States.

Although there is no common agreement on allocation of the marine resources of the high seas, it cannot be ignored that the principle of a preferential share for the coastal State has met with acceptance among a number of States. After the closing of the Conference, the Peruvian delegate circulated among the participants a memorandum which reads in part:

Fortunately, as an ideological and moral compensation for that failure, many delegations have repeatedly advocated the preferential rights of the coastal State to the fisheries in its adjacent sea and the principle of an exception in favour of countries which are in a special situation. This recognition will make a deep mark on contemporary international law and lead to a decisive new step forward in the development of the law of the sea.[17]

Whether the conclusions of the Peruvian delegate are accepted or not, the new direction taken by his memorandum is something to be reckoned with.

(iii) Free Competition vs. Arbitrary Allocation

In principle, two diametrically opposed policies are conceivable for the allocation of fishery resources of the high seas. One, which still finds considerable support, is to leave all the States to compete among themselves to fish freely within the prescribed limits, of course, in a way consonant with the objectives of conservation. The other is an arbitrary allocation based, say, on preferential shares for those States entitled to certain historical preferences or for certain privileged States such as coastal nations. Although there is no general agreement supporting an arbitrary allocation of fishery resources of the high

---

17. UN Doc. A/CONF. 19/L.16.

seas, it is apparent that such a concept will be inevitably crystallised, whenever the stock of fish is so completely exploited that intensive regulation, involving, perhaps, limitations on total catch, would be needed to keep the fish stock from being extinguished. (See table 8.[18])

TABLE 8. SHARING OF HIGH SEAS FISHERY RESOURCES

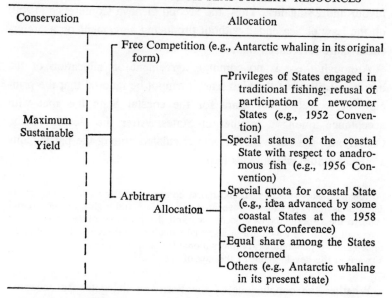

Conservation	Allocation
Maximum Sustainable Yield	Free Competition (e.g., Antarctic whaling in its original form)
	Arbitrary Allocation — Privileges of States engaged in traditional fishing: refusal of participation of newcomer States (e.g., 1952 Convention) — Special status of the coastal State with respect to anadromous fish (e.g., 1956 Convention) — Special quota for coastal State (e.g., idea advanced by some coastal States at the 1958 Geneva Conference) — Equal share among the States concerned — Others (e.g., Antarctic whaling in its present state)

It would be difficult, however, to devise a system of arbitrary allocation which would find universal approval. Free competition is hardly the ideal solution under present circumstances, where the demands of a nation do not necessarily coincide with its ability to fulfill its expectations. On the other hand, the international community does not provide for any supranational authority to assure the various States of a fixed or guaranteed participation on a reasonable basis and in terms of the common interests of the world community. Although free competition is not the ideal solution, it would be imprudent to scrap that principle, one of the most fundamental and well-grounded rationales in modern society, and to substitute a system which would merely give lip-service to so-called "equitable" quotas

18. This table was originally presented in 1963 by the author in his paper, written in Japanese, on the abstention formula.

for fishery resources of the high seas. This is hardly an age of consensus among nations on the general interests of the world community; nor is it likely that any State would be ready to sacrifice its own interests for the benefit of the world at large.

The author wishes to point out only that it is premature to discard the basic principle of free competition accepted in many fields by modern history and to replace it with any principle supporting the arbitrary allocation of fishery resources for the benefit of some historically or geographically privileged States. Few will doubt that, until the time comes when, as in the municipal society, some superauthority can guarantee an equitable sharing of resources among the nations, the States will continue to argue for adoption of principles most favourable to their own interests in the field of high-seas fishing.

In this respect, the theory of international management of high-seas fisheries may be worth noting.[19] It was recently suggested either that a new international body be established or that an existing international organisation, such as the Food and Agriculture Organisation, be empowered to issue licences for high-seas fishing and to collect rentals in return. Issuing licences either to States or to individuals and collecting royalties or fees in return would clearly raise very difficult political or legal problems. And these problems might be overwhelming even where the objective is maximum net economic yields for the world community. The reasons are obvious:

First, the concept of paying "rent" for fishing rights on the high seas, even to an international body, is one unknown (at least for many years) to international law. Except as may have been prescribed by international agreement solely for the purpose of conserving resources from depletion, high-seas fishing has been always free under the time-honoured principle of freedom of the high seas. There is no "landlord of the high seas" authorised to permit or to withhold fishing rights.

Second, if licences should be allocated among the highest bidders, a greater advantage would accrue to the more sophisticated fishing

---

19. See FAO, *The State of Food and Agriculture 1967*, Chapter IV: The Management of Fishery Resources, pp. 119-144.

countries or industries and developing countries wishing to increase their fish supply would be disproportionately restricted.

Third, if not the highest bid, what criterion or criteria should be employed for assigning licences to each applicant? Should priority be given to the nation which may have an historical claim based on its fishing activities over past years, or should it be granted to the State closest to the fisheries?

Should any special consideration be paid to the needs of a specific country, such as a developing nation which lacks a supply of animal protein? But if that is to be a criterion, it must be noted that the purpose of fishing may not be only to provide animal protein food-stuff for a country, but may, more importantly, be aimed at acquiring foreign exchange or profits and expanding employment opportunities.

It is thus extremely difficult to devise any definitive criteria for the allocation of licences or the assignment of permission to fish on the high seas.

3. Geneva Convention on High-Seas Fisheries

Using the draft of the International Law Commission, the 1958 Geneva Conference on the Law of the Sea adopted a Convention on Fishing and Conservation of the Living Resources of the High Seas by 45 votes in favour to 1 against, with 18 abstentions. But it was not until the latest of the four Geneva Conventions on the law of the sea, that this Convention became effective, and this was on 20 March 1966. So far, 28 States (including such maritime States as the United Kingdom and the United States) have ratified or acceded to it. (See table 2.) There is obviously still considerable resistance to the Convention.

For the past ten years, this Convention has been all but neglected in practice, and there are few instances of international agreements or of national legislation in which this Convention is noted. This, in the author's view, is simply because the Convention did not attempt to offer any solution to the real issue which now must be faced in connection with high-seas fisheries, that is, the distribution and allocation of fishery resources among the nations, all of whom will undoubtedly clamour for greater shares for themselves. Nevertheless, it is appropriate at this juncture at least to consider some of the fundamental points of this Convention.

(a) Duty of Conservation

First, inherent in this Convention is the concept of conservation. The Convention provides that a State whose nationals are engaged in fishing any stock of fish shall adopt, for its own nationals, measures for the conservation of such stock, and that, if the nationals of two or more States are engaged in fishing the same stock, these States shall enter into negotiation with a view to arriving at an agreement to prescribe for their respective nationals, the necessary measures for the conservation of the stock. It is an established principle that the fishing State or States may apply conservation measures solely to its or their own nationals. An established conservation programme may be rendered ineffective, however, by the participation of nationals of a State newly entering into the fishing of the stock without any commitment to observe existing regulations. The Convention provides, therefore, that the newcomer State is to apply to its own nationals the existing measures which have been taken by other fishing States. This provision should not be construed as permitting the fishing State or States to exercise jurisdiction over the nationals of the newcomer States. On the contrary, the newcomer State is bound to enforce existing conservation measures as against its own nationals. This heavy obligation is imposed upon all the States adhering to this Convention—a revolutionary concept crystallised by the Convention solely to conserve, as effectively as possible, fishery resources of the high seas.

The duties of the newcomer State are undoubtedly appropriate and desirable in principle. However, the relevant provisions are somewhat complicated, if not outright confusing. A newcomer State is obliged to apply to its own nationals the same conservation measures taken by a fishing State adherent to the Convention. In point of fact, however, a fishing State, when adopting regulations for its nationals, is not likely to anticipate the appearance on the scene of foreign nationals. Furthermore, it is not only conservation of the resources alone, but domestic policies on control of markets and prices as well, which will

61

dictate the nature of regulations on fisheries. It is sometimes very difficult to distinguish regulations intended only for conservation from those emanating from the social or economic policies of a State. Moreover, in certain countries fishing is sometimes controlled in terms of total allowable catch based on the number of licensed fishing vessels in operation. The Convention provision is clearly unworkable in such a case.

(b) Special Interests of the Coastal State

The Convention also sets forth a new concept of the special interests of the coastal State. The coastal State, whose nationals may not even be engaged in fishing off its coasts (beyond its national jurisdiction), is entitled to participate with other fishing States in any conservation measure applicable to off-shore fisheries. The width of these off-shore areas in which the coastal State is entitled to claim special interests is nowhere provided for in the Convention. The coastal State is also empowered to adopt unilateral measures under certain circumstances, but the expression "adopt unilateral measures" (Article 5) should not be construed as enabling the coastal State to extend its control directly over nationals of other States. The Convention did not disturb the established rule of freedom of the high seas, under which a person need observe only the law of his own flagnation. Fishing States are obliged to apply to their own nationals the measures unilaterally adopted by the coastal State, so far as acts within the off-shore areas are concerned.

The provisions on the special interests of the coastal State are subject to differing interpretations, but they should not be read as entitling any States to preferential fishing rights on the basis of their special situation as coastal States. Nor does the Convention impart to the coastal State any power directly to regulate nationals of other fishing States. In fact, the provisions concerning the interests of the coastal State, inserted into the Convention at the suggestion of some of the delegates to the 1958 Conference, are somewhat ambiguous, these delegates having confused the concept of conservation with fishing rights themselves. In spite of the divergent interpretations by and conflicting expectations of the various delegates, it is submitted that all the provisions concerning unilateral measures were drafted to require fishing States to apply to their own nationals, in certain unusual cases, conservation measures unilaterally prescribed by the coastal State.

(c) Compulsory Settlement of Disputes

Third, the Convention contains provisions on compulsory settlement of differences among the States concerning the conservation of fishery resources. Many delegates to the 1958 Conference raised strong objections to the concept of compulsory settlement of disputes. A sharp conflict arose during the earlier stages of the Conference between the States favouring this procedure and those opposing it. The delegates of the United States and of almost all the Western European countries considered compulsory settlement of disputes as an important and even indispensable element, especially in view of the fact that the new concept of "special interests" of the coastal State, which had been theretofore unknown to international law, was about to be recognised. On the other hand, the delegates from the Asian and Latin American nations maintained that they could not accept compulsory arbitration. The States of the Soviet bloc took a similar stand. The procedure was adopted, however, at that Conference with 38 votes in favour, 14 against, and 10 abstentions. The provision calls for the establishment of *ad hoc* commissions, to be known as "special commissions". In the case of parties to the Convention, resort to the special commissions is obligatory and the decisions of these bodies are binding upon the disputants. There are no exceptions to these requirements for compulsory arbitration.

A special commission will be convened only to pass upon the necessity of conservation and the reasonableness of concrete conservation measures. It will not consider other kinds of disputes concerning high-seas fisheries. Determination of conflicting claims to jurisdiction over high-seas fisheries, as well as those relating to the distribution of certain limited marine resources, does not fall within the competence of a special commission.

Taken as a whole, the Geneva Convention on High-Seas Fisheries contains a number of shortcomings, and it is, therefore, not likely that this Convention will in the near future play the role expected of it in 1958.

SUPPLEMENT TO CHAPTER II

*1. Aftermath of the Geneva Convention on High
Seas Fisheries and the Present Position
of Some Fishery Treaties*

The author's criticisms of the Geneva Convention on High Seas Fisheries have already been expressed in his original text and he does not find it necessary to alter these views in any way. He said: "For the past ten years, this Convention has been all but rejected in practice and there are a few instances of international agreements or international legislation in which this Convention is noted" (p. 60). The only alteration to be made here is to say that so far this remains an accurate statement of the position which has continued to exist since the original text appeared ten years ago. It is not intended to follow the various fisheries treaties mentioned in the original text, but it may be necessary to comment briefly on some of them in connection with the author's argument in favour of "distribution" instead of "conservation".

Under the abstention formula of the 1952 North Pacific Fisheries Convention, Japan has been required to abstain from salmon fishing east of the provisional line of longitude 175°W., while the United States has been entitled to full utilization of these resources. The longstanding complaint of Japan, on the ground that Japanese fishing had been placed in a disadvantageous position, has not been resolved, but the *raison d'être* of this Convention has been completely changed due to the establishment of the 200-mile fishery zone in 1976 by the United States. The United States once denounced this Convention in February 1977, thus invalidating the treaty in February 1978.[1] This denunciation was withdrawn by the United States in February 1978, when the three parties to the Convention, Canada, Japan and the United States, agreed upon a new formula under which the provisional line along longitude 175°W. was to be moved to longitude 175°E. and was unfavourable to Japan, but allowed Japanese fishing vessels engaged in salmon fishing into the 200-mile fishing zone of the Aleutian Islands west of the new line of longitude 175°W., but under certain restrictions in terms of the number of fishing vessels and fishing seasons.[2]

On the other hand, the catch of salmon by the Japanese fishing industry in the North West Pacific has been totally dependent on the decision of the Japanese-Soviet Fisheries Commission. The area where Japanese high seas salmon fishing is prohibited has been enlarged, and in 1973 Japanese salmon fishing was totally excluded from the Okhotsk Sea and the permitted catch of salmon, as determined by the Japanese-Soviet

---

1. See *International Legal Materials,* Vol. 16 (1977), p. 1577.
2. See *ibid.,* Vol. 17 (1978), p. 786; *The Asahi,* 11 February 1978.

Fisheries Commission, has gradually decreased, while Soviet salmon fishing in the rivers of the Soviet Union was not affected by the decision of the Commission. The 1956 North West Pacific Fisheries Convention which established this formula lost its meaning as a result of the establishment by the Soviet Union of the 200-mile fishery zone in 1976. This Convention became invalid in April 1978 as a result of its denunciation by the Soviet Union in April 1977.[3] The new Convention between Japan and the Soviet Union to strengthen the co-operation between these two nations for conservation and rational utilization of fishery resources, including salmon, in the areas beyond 200 miles from the coast was agreed in 1978.[4] The Protocol, which was signed the same day, provided a permitted catch for Japan of 42,500 tons in 1978, and also the prohibition of salmon fishing west of longitude 170°E. and north of latitude 44°N. It was also agreed, but on a non-governmental basis, that the Japanese fishing industry would give some aid to the conservation and increased production of salmon stock in terms of equipment as compensation for fishing the stock which breeds in Russian rivers.

Separately from these arrangements, continued fishing by Japanese in the United States' 200-mile fishery zone and the Soviet Union's 200-mile fishery zone is regulated by bilateral agreements which Japan concluded with the United States and the Soviet Union respectively in 1977.[5]

The scheme of free competition within the limit of the total allowable catch in Antarctic whaling had already collapsed nearly twenty years ago and was replaced by a formula for sharing the limited allowable catch among the few interested States. This formula still remains in existence amongst a few nations. Due to the growing movement for the protection of sea animals and also the estimate by scientists warning of the ever-decreasing stock, it is likely that in a few years' time Antarctic whaling will have to cease. The 1957 Fur Seals Convention which provided a unique formula concerning the sharing of the land-based catch of fur seals among Canada, Japan, the Soviet Union and the United States has been extended until 1980.[6] However, it is unlikely that this scheme, which is based on the concept of protection of acquired rights, will be retained for much longer after 1980.

2. High Seas Fisheries Under the Informal Composite Negotiating Text

The regime of the high seas has been established through a long history of the oceans and the 1958 Geneva Convention on the High Seas was

---

3. See *Bulletin of Legal Developments,* 1977, No. 9.
4. *Keizai to Gaiko* (Economy and Diplomacy), No. 672 (May 1978).
5. *International Legal Materials,* Vol. 16 (1977), p. 287; *Japanese Annual of International Law,* Vol. 21 (1977).
6. See Oda, *The International Law of the Ocean Development,* p. IX.D.i.2/76.

regarded as reflecting customary international law. There have been no great changes in this area. However, we must note the following points in connection with fishing in the high seas.

First of all, parallel to the establishment of exclusive economic zones, the area of the high seas will be diminished. The size of the high seas is no longer the same as it was in 1958. Secondly, as far as highly migratory species are concerned, which will remain practically as the sole high seas fishery resource, there will be fewer species in the high seas for fishermen. Thirdly, and most important of all, the concept of the freedom of fishing on the high seas has been changing. Freedom of fishing has undoubtedly been considered one of the basic freedoms for many centuries. Today, however, fishing in the high seas is placed under some restrictions. Demands have often been made to drop fishing from the list of the freedoms of the high seas. Such demands were made at the Third Law of the Sea Conference and Article 87 of the Informal Composite Negotiating Text[7] mentions the freedom of fishing as being "subject to the conditions" specified in Articles 116 to 120 of that Text. In addition, in 1958, the High Seas Fisheries Convention was drafted simply as a supplement to the high seas regime but, today, conservation and management of fishery resources is an integral part of the regime of the high seas now covered by one instrument.

The author finds many shortcomings and contradictions in the provisions relating to high seas fisheries in the Text. First of all Article 116 provides that the right to fish is subject to "the rights and duties as well as the interest of coastal States provided for, *inter alia*, in" the provision of the exclusive economic zone covering "stocks occurring within the exclusive economic zones of two or more coastal States or both within the exclusive economic zone and in an area beyond and adjacent to it" (Article 63), "highly migratory species" (Article 64), "marine mammals" (Article 65), "anadromous stocks" (Article 66), and "catadromous species" (Article 67). However, it should be asked whether there are any *other* "rights and duties as well as interests of coastal States" which are recognized in the Text. It must be noted that this Text is different from the 1958 Convention which, without putting forward the concept of the exclusive economic zone, provided that the coastal State was entitled to have some special or preferential rights in its coastal areas. Apart from the case of some species specifically mentioned, the coastal State is not granted, under this Text, any special competence or rights in fisheries beyond the exclusive economic zone.

Secondly, Article 118 suggests "co-operation of States in the management and conservation of living resources". Strangely enough, the concept of management of the living resources of the high seas does not appear earlier in the Text. It is true that this concept was applied in a document prepared by the FAO in 1967, as the author has already pointed out (page 59). The author's concern for "distribution and allo-

---

7. UN Doc. A/CONF.62/WP.10 and Add. 1.

66

cation" of the resources of the high seas is also a relevant concept. Yet, the problem of management was not discussed at the Third Conference of the Law of the Sea. The Text simply adopts the word "management" without suggesting any concrete content for the concept. Though the first sentence of Article 118 mentions co-operation of States in the management of living resources in addition to their conservation, the idea of management disappears as from the second sentence of the same article.

Thirdly, the concept of conservation of fishery resources in the high seas also seems to be ill-defined in the Text. Article 119, which provides for the concept of conservation, states that "in determining the allowable catch and establishing other conservation measures for the living resources in the high seas, States shall . . ." be placed under certain obligations. However, no duty to determine the allowable catch or to establish other conservation measures is provided for in this Text. In addition, paragraph 3 of this Article provides for the duty of States to ensure that "conservation measures and their implementation do not discriminate in form or in fact against fishermen of any State". This provision also seems to be based on some misconception of the competence of the coastal State. Certainly a similar provision is found in the 1958 Convention in which the possibility of regulation by the coastal State in offshore areas was conceded in the light of the concept of a special interest of the coastal State. On the other hand, under this Text, apart from those provisions which have already been referred to, there does not seem to exist any interest of the coastal State in high seas fisheries, and the implementation of the conservation measures for high seas fisheries will only be on the basis of the consent of the State concerned by means to be agreed. There can be no possibility of implementing measures which will discriminate "in form or in fact" against foreign fishermen under this formula of agreed regulation of high seas fisheries, except in cases where the States concerned are willing to agree thereto. This provision thus makes little sense.

Fourthly, Article 120 concerning marine mammals does not make any sense at all, since Article 65 which is quoted in that Article is intended to suggest that, in spite of the fundamental principle of full utilization of the living resources within the exclusive economic zone, the coastal States or international organizations may prescribe, regulate and limit the exploitation of marine mammals in that area. There is no ground for applying this provision to the exploitation of marine mammals of the high seas as suggested in Article 120.

CHAPTER III

SPECIAL TREATMENT OF SEDENTARY FISHERIES

(a) The Problems in General

Sedentary fish, although they may be considered a category of fishery resources, have been treated, in legal respects, quite separately from ordinary fish. It is submitted that, at the Geneva Conference, a serious error was made in connection with the Continental Shelf Convention provision on the definition of continental shelf resources. As contemplated by the Convention, the continental shelf resources include not only mineral resources but also certain kinds of sedentary fisheries, that is to say, "organisms which, at the harvestable stage, either are immobile on or under the seabed or are unable to move except in constant physical contact with the seabed".

This treatment of sedentary fisheries independently of regular fishing and jointly with the seabed appears to be justified only by certain past practices.[1] For example, in the case of Ceylon, Tunisia and Bahrein, recognition has been granted to jurisdictional assertions by the coastal State over such marine products as pearl shell, coral, and sponge. Apart from this historical exception, no logical reason exists for viewing the exploitation of resources attached to the seabed in terms of the legal status of submerged lands in general. The questions should not be whether the resources swim in the ocean or are attached to the seabed but, rather, what human activities are required for their exploitation. Since both types of fishing are carried out in the high seas, the exploitation of resources attached to the seabed is no different from regular fishing, and there is no reason why the same rules of law should not apply to both. The sedentary fisheries pertain to the high seas rather than to the seabed. No scholar has been able convincingly to justify either the exclusion of sedentary

---

1. Hurst, Sir Cecil, "Whose is the Bed of the Sea?", *British Year Book of International Law,* Vol. 4, 1923/24, pp. 34-43.

fisheries from the general regime of the high seas or their inclusion in the regime of the seabed. Except for particular banks, where fishing has been carried on since time immemorial, it has not been found necessary to treat the exploitation of resources attached to the seabed any differently from ordinary fishing. From a policy standpoint, too, there is no logic in differentiating authority over fishing operations on the basis of *what* is caught or *how* it is caught.[2]

The error of the Convention may be traced to the International Law Commission in 1953, which had come to the conclusion that the products of sedentary fisheries should not be excluded from the operation of the regime of the continental shelf. At the Geneva Conference, many European countries insisted that the definition of continental shelf resources be limited to mineral resources, while some of the Asian countries maintained that even bottom fish, such as halibut, should be included in the category of continental shelf resources. To reach a compromise between the two opposing views, a new proposal was submitted including among the continental shelf resources certain sedentary species but explicitly excluding crustacea therefrom. For sponsoring States intended to differentiate between the mineral and sedentary resources, on the one hand, and fishery resources, including crustacea and bottom fish, on the other. The United Kingdom delegate explained, in support of the joint proposal, that the recommendation was submitted only with a view to bringing the conference to a successful conclusion, even though the proposal might be disadvantageous to his own Government.[3] The concept of sedentary fisheries as continental shelf resources was accepted by the Geneva Conference, the exclusion of crustacea having been dropped from that category of sea life.

Today, the coastal State is entitled under the Convention to exert control over oyster beds and pearl fisheries. The International Law Commission's deliberations and the Conference's discussions make it clear, however, that all the provisions of the Convention were drafted principally to apply only to the exploitation of mineral resources of

---

2. This view was presented by the author in Oda, S., "A Reconsideration of the Continental Shelf Doctrine", *Tulane Law Review*, Vol. 32, 1957, pp. 21-36.
3. *UN Conference on the Law of the Sea, 1958*, Vol. VI, p. 61.

submerged lands and not to sedentary fishery resources. The history of this provision provides no basis for the belief that, either as *lex lata* or *lex ferenda,* sedentary fisheries were intended to be treated in the same manner as the mineral resources of the continental shelf.

(b) Problems of the King Crab

(i) Interpretation of the Geneva Convention

A very complicated problem has arisen with regard to sedentary species. The relevant provision of the Convention now seems to permit two contradictory interpretations of the status of crustacea because, at some point during the drafting of the Convention the proposed exclusion of crustacea from sedentary fisheries was overlooked. It should be recalled that at Geneva the delegate of Australia, in introducing the compromise proposal, made it clear that crustacea, including all species of crabs, should not fall within "sedentary fisheries".[4] The following interpretation presented to the United States Senate by Arthur Dean, Chairman of the United States delegation, is also relevant in this respect: " . . . clams, oysters, abalone, etc., are included in the definition [of 'natural resources'], whereas shrimp, lobsters, and finny fish are not".[5] Certainly, Mr. Dean did not refer to all the various species to be categorised as continental shelf resources. He did not, however, specify king crab as a resource to be excluded therefrom. In fact, shrimp and lobster, as well as king crab, belong to the decapoda branch of crustacea. It seems quite reasonable to assume that, although a literal interpretation of the provision would permit the opposite inference, Mr. Dean intended to exclude crustacea, or at least decapoda, from the category of continental shelf resources, while clams, oysters, and abalone were to be included.

A few nations have taken positions on the interpretation of sedentary species to be included among continental shelf resources. But France is the only country to make an explicit pronouncement on the relevant provision of the Convention. France, on depositing the

---

4. *Id.,* p. 56.
5. US, *Hearing on Exec. J.K.L.M.N. Before the Senate Committee on Foreign Relations,* 86th Cong., 2d Sess. (20 January 1960), p. 88.

instrument of accession to the Convention in 1965, declared that "the Government of the French Republic considers that the expression 'living organisms belonging to sedentary species' must be interpreted as excluding crustaceous".

On the other hand, a completely opposite stand was recently taken by the United States and the USSR. The United States, in 1964 legislation prohibiting foreign vessels from fishing in territorial waters and on the continental shelf, deems it unlawful for foreign vessels to engage in the taking of any continental shelf fishery resources of the United States.[6] The term "continental shelf fishery resources" is defined in this Act to include the living resources designated as continental shelf resources under the Geneva Convention. In signing this legislation, the President made it clear that king crab would be covered by this definition. The United States Department of Interior in October 1968 promulgated a list of the continental shelf resources covered by the Act of 1964. In it king crab and tanner crab were included.[7] The United States has thus apparently altered its position with regard to crustacea, and it now includes crustacea in the list of continental shelf resources. The USSR acted similarly through a decree of the Soviet Supreme Presidium of 6 February 1968, which explicitly stated that sedentary species were included among resources of the continental shelf.[8] In January 1969, the USSR Ministry of Fisheries published a list of these resources, and included therein king crab and tanner crab.

(ii) United States-USSR Agreement of 1965

In 1965, the United States and the USSR concluded an agreement relating to fishing for king crab on the United States continental shelf extending under the eastern Bering Sea.[9] Both Governments, which had ratified the Continental Shelf Convention, agreed that "the king crab is a natural resource of the continental shelf". However, in view of ongoing Russian king crab fishing in the eastern Bering Sea, the United States agreed that nationals and vessels of the USSR might

---

6. *International Legal Materials,* Vol. 3, 1964, p. 642.
7. *US Federal Register,* Vol. 33, No. 215 (2 November 1968).
8. *International Legal Materials,* Vol. 7, 1968, p. 392.
9. *UN Treaty Series,* Vol. 541, p. 97.

carry out commercial fishing for king crab along certain specified areas of the United States continental shelf.

(iii) Japan-United States Agreement of 1964

In contrast to these amicable arrangements between the United States and the USSR, the negotiations between Japan and the United States were difficult, since Japan, like France, maintains that, if a sedentary living resource is to be included in continental shelf resources, the king crab certainly should not be considered such a sedentary resource. For practical reasons only, Japan, which had lodged a strong protest with the United States Government when the 1964 legislation on continental shelf resources was submitted to the United States Congress, had reached an agreement with the United States late in 1964 regarding fishing for king crab in the eastern Bering Sea.[10] The understanding made it clear that, while the Japanese Government considered king crab to be a high seas fishery resource, the United States adhered to the view that the king crab was a natural resource of the continental shelf over which the United States had exclusive jurisdiction, control and rights of exploitation. Under this two-year accord, both Governments agreed, without prejudicing their respective positions, that king crab fishing carried out by Japanese on the United States continental shelf in the eastern Bering Sea might continue. This agreement was extended in 1966 and again in 1968 for successive two-year periods.

(iv) Japan-USSR Agreement of 1969

Negotiations between Japan and the USSR on Japanese fishing of king crab off the coasts of Kamtschatka also reached a fruitful conclusion in April 1969. It is explicitly stated in this agreement, which was effective only during 1969, that this practical solution for the continuation by Japanese of fishing king crab off the coasts of Kamtschatka affirms neither the Russian position that the king crab is a natural resource of the continental shelf nor the Japanese posture that the king crab must be considered a fishery resource of the high seas.

---

10. *Id.*, Vol. 533, p. 31.

On analysis, there seems to be no reason why the United States and the USSR need compound the error of the Geneva Conference by extending the scope of the continental shelf resources to cover crustacea, which, unlike pearl shell, sponges, etc., are in no wise permanently attached to the seabed.

(c) Recommendations

The author's first recommendation is that the consolidated treatment of sedentary fisheries and the continental shelf should be excised from the Continental Shelf Convention, since it is plain that there is no logical or historical basis for a uniform treatment of these two disparate problems.

If, however, this blunderbuss approach is retained for no reason other than convenience, the author then recommends that such crustacea as king crab should be expressly excluded from the category of continental shelf resources; and the regime of the high seas relating to fishing, certain international regulations on the conservation of fishery resources, and, especially, the Geneva Convention on Fishing and Conservation of the Living Resources of the High Seas, should all be made applicable to sedentary fisheries and the fishing of king crab in particular. The author reiterates that there is no reason for these living resources to be treated differently from ordinary fishery resources and handled in the same way as petroleum or natural gas (which require completely different operations) on the sole ground that these living resources crawl on the seabed and do not swim in the sea.

SUPPLEMENT TO CHAPTER III

The author does not find it necessary to change his position with regard
to sedentary fisheries which should be regarded as separate from the
regime of the continental shelf and understood as one type of fishing.
Past practice indicates, however, that in some cases, sedentary fisheries
have been regulated under regional agreements which are quite separate
from those covering ordinary fishing. It may, of course, be true that as
200-mile exclusive economic zones are being established it would not be
proper to treat sedentary fisheries as a part of high sea fishing, as
suggested previously by the author. However, it may be that under the
new regime sedentary fisheries within the 200-mile limit should be
treated as part of fishing in the exclusive economic zone and should
come under Articles 61 and 62 of the Informal Composite Negotiating
Text,[1] while sedentary fisheries beyond that limit should be placed under
the high seas regime, and in this case Articles 116 to 119 should apply.
But, in fact, the Text makes provision for sedentary fisheries in a quite
different way. Article 68 suggests that the regime of the exclusive economic zone will never apply to sedentary fisheries and that, as in the
1958 Continental Shelf Convention, they should instead be regarded
as part of the natural resources of the continental shelf; that, in other
words, the concept of full utilization or conservation suggested for the
exclusive economic zone will never apply to sedentary fisheries. On the
other hand, the sovereign right of the coastal State to sedentary fisheries
will, parallel to the outer limit of the continental shelf, extend beyond
200 miles from the coast in some cases. The author would like to
restate his original reservations that it would be illogical, politically,
economically and scientifically, to separate sedentary fisheries from
ordinary fishing and combine them with the regime of the seabed. He
still does not understand the rationale behind the provision concerning
sedentary fisheries, neither in the 1958 Convention nor in the new Text.

---

1. UN Doc. A/CONF.62/WP.10 and Add. 1.

PART II

INTERNATIONAL LAW RELATING TO MARINE MINERAL RESOURCES

A shelf extending at a certain depth below the sea exists along continental coasts. The name given to this projection, the continental shelf, is new neither to the geologist nor to the lawyer. About 20 years ago the possibility of profitably working the resources, especially petroleum, contained in this shelf became a subject of world-wide attention. A number of States thereupon lay claim to their respective off-shore submerged areas with a view to securing the resources which they contained.

Yet the areas lying beyond the continental shelf have received serious discussion only in the past few years, and this mainly through the initiative which Ambassador Pardo, permanent representative of Malta to the United Nations, took at the United Nations General Assembly in 1967.

At present, there are in existence two quite distinct regimes relating to these two submarine areas: one, the continental shelf regime, which has already clothed itself with considerable background and substance in the rule of international law; and the other, a completely new regime, which is now being discussed at great length in the United Nations and also by various non-governmental organisations.

CHAPTER IV

REGIME OF THE CONTINENTAL SHELF

1. The Continental Shelf Convention

In 1945 the United States, under the now well-known Truman Proclamation, claimed the submarine areas off its coasts with the statement: "the Government of the United States regards the natural resources of the subsoil and seabed of the continental shelf beneath the high seas but contiguous to the coasts of the United States as appertaining to the United States, subject to its jurisdiction and control".[1] Suggesting a 100-fathom depth as determinative of the continental shelf limit, the United States clearly intended to prevent other States from drawing near the United States coast for the purpose of exploiting submarine resources. Many other coastal States followed this precedent, undoubtedly because, in doing so, they had much to gain and nothing to lose. In this context, some States have asserted that the continental shelf forms part of their national territory, while others have claimed limited jurisdiction over the shelf for the purpose of exploitation of its resources. And still others have asserted ownership of the resources contained in the continental shelf. All of these claimants, however, one way or another, have asserted an exclusive right to certain limited areas of the subsoil beneath the high seas.[2]

While the regime of the continental shelf as *lex lata* has been discussed by many scholars primarily from the theoretical point of view, the United Nations International Law Commission endeavoured to establish a *lex ferenda* for the exclusive exploitation of submarine resources. In 1950, in his first report on the high seas, Professor François, who had been appointed special rapporteur on the topic of the regime of the high seas, devoted one-fourth of the entire

---

1. *American Journal of International Law,* Vol. 40, 1946, Supplement, p. 45.
2. See UN Documents referred to in note 10, at p. 7.

TABLE 9. ATTITUDES OF THE STATES TOWARD THE REGIME OF THE CONTINENTAL SHELF (as of 1 August 1969)

	Continental Shelf Convention: (Ratification or Accession)	Domestic Measures
Asia		
Cambodia	18 Mar. 1960	1957
Ceylon	—	1957: proclamation
India	—	1959: rule
Indonesia	—	11 Feb. 1969: proclamation
Iran	—	19 June 1955: act
Iraq	—	10 Apr. 1958: proclamation
Israel	6 Sep. 1961	3 Aug. 1952: proclamation
Korea (Rep. of)	—	18 Jan. 1952: proclamation
Kuwait	—	12 June 1949
Malaysia	21 Dec. 1960	28 July 1966: act
Pakistan	—	9 Mar. 1950: proclamation
Philippines	—	20 Mar. 1968
Saudi Arabia	—	28 May 1949: royal decree
Thailand	2 July 1968	7 Sep. 1968:
Viet-Nam (South)	—	1967
Oceania		
Australia	14 May 1963	22 Nov. 1967: act
New Zealand	18 Jan. 1965	3 Nov. 1964: act
Africa		
Dahomey	—	7 Mar. 1968: decree (100 miles)
Ghana	—	19 Apr. 1963: act; 27 Nov. 1968: amended
Ivory Coast	—	1 Aug. 1967: decree
Kenya	20 June 1969	
Madagascar	31 July 1962	
Malawi	3 Nov. 1965	
Mauritania	—	1967
Senegal	25 April 1961	21 June 1961: act
Sierra Leone	25 Nov. 1966	
South Africa (Rep.)	9 April 1963	29 June 1963: act
Uganda	14 Sep. 1964	
United Arab Rep.	—	3 Sep. 1958: decree
Western Europe		
Belgium	—	11 Oct. 1967: draft legislation
Denmark	12 June 1963	7 June 1963: royal decree
Finland	16 Feb. 1965	5 Mar. 1965: act
France	14 June 1965	1965
Germany (Fed. Rep.)	—	22 Jan. 1964: proclamation
Italy	—	21 July 1967: act
Malta	19 May 1966	1966
Netherlands	18 Feb. 1966	23 Sep. 1965: act
Norway	—	21 June 1963: act
Portugal	8 Jan. 1963	21 Mar. 1956: act

80

Spain	—		26 Dec. 1958: act
Sweden	1 June	1966	3 June 1966: act
Switzerland	18 May	1966	
U.K.	11 May	1964	15 Apr. 1964: act

Eastern Europe

Albania	7 Dec.	1964	
Bulgaria	31 Aug.	1962	
Byelorussian SSR	27 Jan.	1961	
Czechoslovakia	31 Aug.	1961	
Germany (East)	—		23 Oct. 1968: joint proclamation
Poland	29 June	1962	23 Oct. 1968: joint proclamation
Romania	12 Dec.	1961	1961
Ukrainian SSR	12 Feb.	1961	
U.S.S.R.	22 Nov.	1960	6 Feb. 1968: decree; 23 Oct.
			1968: proclamation
Yugoslavia	28 Jan.	1966	22 May 1965: act

North America

U.S.	12 Apr.	1961

Latin America

Argentina	—		29 Dec. 1966: act
Brazil	—		26 Aug. 1968: decree
Chile	—		23 June 1947: proclamation
Colombia	8 Jan.	1962	
Costa Rica	—		**1961**
Dominican Rep.	11 Aug.	1964	2 Nov. 1949: decree
Ecuador	—		6 Sep. 1967: act
El Salvador	—		20 Aug. 1960: civil code
Guatemala	27 Nov.	1961	7 Sep. 1950: constitution
Guyana	—		26 Sep. 1965: constitution
Haiti	29 Mar.	1960	1954
Honduras	—		1965
Jamaica	8 Oct.	1965	
Mexico	2 Aug.	1966	1945
Nicaragua	—		1 Nov. 1950: constitution
Panama	—		1 Mar. 1946: constitution
Peru	—		1 Aug. 1947: proclamation
Trinidad-Tobago	11 July	1968	
Uruguay	—		1963
Venezuela	15 Aug.	1961	23 Jan. 1961: constitution

treatment to the question of the continental shelf. From that point on, the question of the continental shelf has been treated by the International Law Commission as one of the most important facets of the regime of the high seas. The concept underlying the regime of the continental shelf has not been materially altered in the course of seven years' debate by the Commission, which, after extensive discussion, had at last, in 1956, completed its draft articles on the subject. At the Geneva Conference of 1958, the Convention on the Continental Shelf was adopted with a vote of 57 in favour, 3 against, and 8 abstentions.

The Continental Shelf Convention became effective on 10 June 1964. By 1 September 1969, the Convention had become binding upon 40 States, including the United Kingdom, the United States and the USSR. (See table 2.) Both developed and developing, and Western and socialist, countries are among the nations adhering to the Convention.

Forty is perhaps not a remarkable number when it is compared with the total figure of nation-States at present existing in the world. On the other hand, many States have enacted domestic legislation in content similar to the Convention. It is indicated in table 9 that certain nations, while not adhering to the Convention, have in general committed themselves to the regime of the continental shelf. It can be said, therefore, that, *in toto,* no fewer than 70 nations have already indicated observance of the regime of the continental shelf.

This does not necessarily mean that all the provisions of the Convention are binding on the States which are not parties to it. All the more true in the light of certain provisions which were inappropriate even at the time the Convention was drafted and of others which have become so with recent developments.

The Convention provides that, five years from its effective date, a request for revision may be made by any contracting party by notifying the United Nations Secretary-General. This five-year period expired only recently; and revision of certain provisions of the Convention, often discussed in and out of the United Nations, is now possible, and even likely.

2. Fundamental Regime of the Continental Shelf

(a) Drafting of the Relevant Provisions of the Convention

The International Law Commission, all during its seven years of deliberations on the problem, never once questioned the advisability of adopting the principle of the continental shelf as *lex ferenda*; and in its final draft (1956) it adopted the following approach to the subject:

> The rights of the coastal State over the continental shelf do not depend on occupation, effective or notional, or on any express proclamation . . . [I]t is not possible to base the sovereign rights of the coastal State exclusively on recent practice, . . . However, that practice itself is considered by the Commission to be supported by considerations of law and of fact . . . [O]nce the seabed and the subsoil have become an object of active interest to coastal States with a view to the exploration and exploitation of their resources, they cannot be considered as *res nullius*, i.e., capable of being appropriated by the first occupier. It is natural that coastal States should resist any such solution . . . [It is not] possible to disregard the geographical phenomenon whatever the term—propinquity, contiguity, geographical continuity, appurtenance or identity—used to define the relationship between the submarine areas in question and the adjacent non-submerged land. All these considerations of general utility provide a sufficient basis for the principle of the sovereign rights of the coastal State, as now formulated by the Commission.[3]

At the 1958 Geneva Conference, several European countries balked at supporting the concept of the continental shelf as set forth in the International Law Commission's draft, but most other States entered into the deliberations without questioning the concept, as a whole, of the continental shelf; and no further disagreement with the fundamental status of this submerged area was heard at the Conference. The Continental Shelf Convention, enunciating for the first time the theory as a positive rule of law, allowed each coastal State to claim exclusive rights of exploitation of the continental shelf off its coast. The basic concept of this new regime is set forth in Article 2, paragraph 1:

> Art. 2, para. 1—The coastal State exercises over the continental shelf sovereign rights for the purpose of exploring it and exploiting its natural resources.

---

3. *Report of the International Law Commission, 1956*, p. 42, art. 68, paras. 7, 8.

This provision is the keystone of the regime of the continental shelf. Whether the rights to be vested in the coastal State should be sovereign or exclusive, was strenuously debated at the Conference. But more important is the *substance* of the rights which the coastal State may enjoy, regardless of whether they be termed sovereign or exclusive.

The fundamental regime of the continental shelf is supplemented by the following provisions of the Convention:

Art. 2, para. 2—The rights referred to in paragraph 1 of this article are exclusive in the sense that if the coastal State does not explore the continental shelf or exploit its natural resources, no one may undertake these activities, or make a claim to the continental shelf, without the express consent of the coastal State.

Para. 3—The rights of the coastal State over the continental shelf do not depend on occupation, effective or notional, or on any express proclamation.

The Convention certainly obviated various theoretical controversies concerning individual claims of many States to their off-shore submarine areas. Thus, in 1958, the road to control of the continental shelf was paved.

(b) The North Sea Continental Shelf Cases

The recent judgment of the International Court of Justice in the North Sea Continental Shelf cases seems to have put an end to discussion of whether the regime of the continental shelf is still a kind of *lex ferenda* or it has been established under customary international law. It is sufficient at this juncture to quote part of the judgment:

The rights of the coastal State in respect of the area of continental shelf that constitutes a natural prolongation of its land territory into and under the sea exist *ipso facto* and *ab initio,* by virtue of its sovereign rights for the purpose of exploring the seabed and exploiting its natural resources. In short, there is here an inherent right. In order to exercise it, no special legal process has to be gone through, nor have any special legal acts to be performed. Its existence can be declared (and many States have done this) but does not need to be constituted. Furthermore, the right does not depend on its being exercised.[4]

There can be no doubt, in the light of this judgment, that the fundamental regime of the continental shelf is now an accepted con-

---

4. *I.C.J. Reports 1969, North Sea Continental Shelf Cases (Federal Republic of Germany/Denmark; Federal Republic of Germany/Netherlands),* p. 22.

cept of customary international law. In other words, each State, whether or not it has ratified or acceded to the Continental Shelf Convention, is entitled to control its own off-shore subsoil areas for the purpose of their exploration and exploitation. The coastal State may enact any regulations it chooses in connection with exploitation of the resources of its continental shelf, and it may apply them to its own or foreign nationals, to whom it may have granted concessions for exploitation of resources.

It should be stressed again, however, that it is only the general concept of the continental shelf and not necessarily the entirety of its provisions, which has been firmly established. Not all States take the same stand as to the extent and boundaries of the continental shelf or the nature of continental shelf resources. For instance, the Court itself stated in its judgment that the equidistance method explicitly provided for in the Convention for drawing the boundary of the continental shelf among neighbouring States does not represent a rule of customary international law.

Despite the development of a body of customary international law on the regime of the continental shelf, there still exist technical problems and problems of detail which must be solved. One problem relates to the geographical extent of the continental shelf over which each State is entitled to claim sovereign rights, the point of demarcation being either the seaward outer edge of the continental shelf or the boundary of the continental shelf among neighbouring States. Second, there is the question of how to reconcile exploitation of the continental shelf with other uses of high seas superjacent to the continental shelf. Third, a further question relates to the legal status of the waters superjacent to the continental shelf.

3. Outer Edge of the Continental Shelf

(a) Drafting of the Relevant Provisions of the Convention

According to the Continental Shelf Convention, the shelf is defined in terms of (1) the depth of the superjacent waters; (2) the concept of adjacency to the coast; and (3) the criterion of exploitability. Article 1 of the Convention reads:

Art. 1—The term "continental shelf" is used as referring ... to the seabed and subsoil of the submarine areas adjacent to the coast ... to a depth of 200 metres or, beyond that limit, to where the depth of the superjacent waters admits of the exploitation of the natural resources of the said areas ...

In 1950 the International Law Commission considered that the legal concept of the continental shelf need not depend on the existence of a geographical continental shelf, where the depth of the superjacent waters permitted exploitation. In the first text on the regime of the continental shelf, as prepared by the Commission at its 1951 session, the continental shelf was defined only in terms of exploitability.[5] The criterion of 200 metres depth, generally considered as the limit of the continental shelf ever since the Truman Proclamation was issued in 1945, was not referred to in the 1951 draft. The Commission considered the possibility of adopting a fixed limit in terms of the depth of the superjacent waters, but felt that a limit of 200 metres depth would become unrealistic if technical developments in the near future should make it possible to exploit resources of the seabed at a depth of over 200 metres. In 1953 the International Law Commission abandoned the criterion of exploitability adopted in 1951 and opted in its 1953 draft for a depth of 200 metres as the only criterion of the limit of the continental shelf.[6] The Commission took the view that the previously adopted text, which did not satisfy the requirement of certainty, might possibly give rise to disputes.

In 1956, however, the Commission again modified its position. In its final draft that year it revised the delineation of the continental shelf to extend to the 200-metre depth and to depend in part on the criterion of exploitability.[7] The rationale of the 200-metre depth has always rested on the fact that the continental shelf (in the geographical sense) generally comes to an end at that point, and it is there that the continental slope begins, with a steep drop to a great depth. But the

---

5. Report of the International Law Commission, 1951, p. 17, art. 1; commentary 6 thereto.
6. Id., 1953, p. 12, art. 1; para. 64.
7. Id., 1956, p. 11, art. 67.

86

record of the drafting of this provision at the International Law Commission leads one to suspect that the Commission had mistakenly assumed that the exploitation of the subsoil would be permissible *only* in terms of claims to the continental shelf. In other words, the International Law Commission seems not to have come to grips with the question of exploitation of resources beyond the 200-metre line. The nub of the concept of the continental shelf, however, is *not* whether its submarine areas can be successfully worked *but* whether the coastal State exercises *exclusive control* over the shelf. This most crucial point was overlooked by the International Law Commission.

As in the case of the International Law Commission, many of the participants in the Geneva Conference of 1958 seemed to confuse the concept of *exclusive control* of resources by the coastal State (in terms of the continental shelf regime) with the concept of *utilisation* of the submarine areas, and several proposals were submitted to the Conference to define the outer limits of the shelf.

The delegates of France, the United Kingdom, Italy and the United States were reluctant to accept the theory that the limit of the continental shelf be determined by such an uncertain criterion as "exploitability". They favoured basing the limitation on a depth of 200 metres.[8] A simple limit of 200 metres was proposed by the French delegation, but it was rejected, and the original draft prepared by the International Law Commission, which combined the 200-metre isobath and the exploitability test, was adopted. The United States and the USSR voted in favour, and France, Germany, Italy, Japan and the Netherlands, among others, voted against. The United Kingdom delegate abstained because she considered that the provision was likely to give rise to uncertainty. In the final stages of the Conference, the French delegate again tried to delete the concept of exploitability from the original text; but the text was adopted unchanged. Thus, the International Law Commission's definition of the continental shelf remained as originally conceived.

---

8. *UN Conference on the Law of the Sea, 1958,* Vol. VI, pp. 1-19.

(b) Interpretation of the Provisions

(i) Exploitability Test

It is not necessary for the coastal State itself to engage in the exploitation of its continental shelf: each coastal State is free to grant to any foreign country or foreign nationals the right to explore its continental shelf or to exploit the natural resources therein contained. It is likely that the developing nations without sufficiently advanced technologies and industries will encourage foreign investment or invite technical assistance with a view towards the exploitation of the resources contained within the submerged areas which they claim. Thus, the concept of exploitability must be constantly reassessed in terms of the most advanced standards of technology and economy in the world; and the exploitation of submarine resources at any point must always be reserved to the coastal State, which alone is empowered to claim the area when the depth of the superjacent waters admits of exploitation.

It can be inferred that, under this Convention, all the submarine areas of the world have been theoretically divided among the coastal States. This is at least one conclusion which may be drawn from the provision approved at the Geneva Conference, although such an interpretation was perhaps not what the delegates at the Geneva Conference thought they were actually affirming.[9] Many delegates at Geneva simply and mistakenly considered that the exploitation of resources had become permissible through the regime of the continental shelf and that the provision on "exploitability" permitted the coastal State to exploit submarine resources even where the depth of the superjacent waters exceeds 200 metres, should this region ever become exploitable.

---

9. This view was presented by the author in Oda, S., *International Control of Sea Resources*, 1963, p. 167. See, also, Münch, F., "Die Internationale Seerechtskonferenze", *Archiv des Völkerrechts*, Bd. 8, 1959, pp. 180, 206; Dreyfus, S., "Considérations sur le Statut Juridique du Plateau Continental et la Conférence de Genève de 1958", *Annuaire de l'A.A.A.*, Vol. 30, 1960, pp. 23, 25.

(ii) Concept of Adjacency

In addition to "exploitability", another criterion, "adjacency" to the coast, is also mentioned in the Continental Shelf Convention. Some efforts have been made in reliance on this latter criterion, to bring a halt to the gradual extension of claims to the continental shelf. Relevant in this respect is the declaration made by the Government of France in 1965 on depositing the instrument of its accession to the effect that "the expression 'adjacent' areas implies a notion of geo-physical, geological and geographical dependence which *ipso facto* rules out an unlimited extension of the continental shelf". It is often pointed out that exploitability should be interpreted in connection with the concept of "adjacent" areas and that an outer limit should be placed on the continental shelf. But whatever proposal may be made in connection with future policy in delimiting the outer limit of the continental shelf on the basis of the "adjacent area" concept, it will be difficult if not impossible to apply this concept in a concrete manner, since the very concept of an "adjacent area" is a relative matter.

The work at the United Nations for the past two years on the peaceful uses of the deep ocean floor seems to have resulted in a general consensus that there should be a precise boundary separating the continental shelf from the area which may require a completely new regime. As a matter of fact, the problem of the outer limit of the continental shelf is now being discussed mainly in terms of a future policy relating to a regime for the deep ocean floor.

4. Boundaries of the Continental Shelf

(a) Relevant Provisions of the Convention

The limitation of the continental shelf assumes a particular importance in areas where the depth of the superjacent waters does not exceed 200 metres and the shelf extends (1) from the territories of two or more States whose coasts are opposite each other, or (2) from the territories of two adjacent States. The Convention provides in Article 6 that the boundary of the shelf in both situations is to be determined by agreement and that, in the absence of agreement, and unless another boundary is justified by special circumstances, the boundary is the line equidistant from the baselines of the States concerned.

The Geneva Convention leaves something to be desired so far as its treatment of the continental shelf boundary line is concerned. First of all, the Convention suggests no criteria for the drawing of boundaries by agreement, and it is extremely likely that, in the absence of objective criteria, any solution by agreement will be largely dependent on political considerations. This is not to say that this approach is impossible. However, to suggest a solution by agreement without any reference to objective criteria would inevitably lead to chaos in most cases. Even where a solution is ultimately reached by agreement, certain criteria should be established in advance as points of departure.

Secondly, while an agreement represents an accord between the parties, it need not exclude the objective determinants of "special circumstances" or the "equidistance line". Boundaries may very well be determined either by agreement or through some form of impartial third-party decision. But in both cases, it is essential that there be criteria to provide guidelines. The real intent of the Continental Shelf Convention seems to be that, whether there is an agreement or some form of third-party decision, either the equidistance line or a line justified by special circumstances should be considered as criteria in setting the boundary of each State's continental shelf.[10]

(b) Equidistance Line

(i) Bilateral Agreements

There are some examples of States reaching bilateral agreement on dividing the continental shelf among themselves. (See table 10.)

The United Kingdom, through various agreements, succeeded in obtaining boundary accords with Norway, Denmark and the Nether-

---

10. See Oda, S., "Proposal for Revising the Convention on the Continental Shelf", *Columbia Journal of Transnational Law*, Vol. 7, 1968, pp. 1, 24.

lands in the North Sea area.[11] Except for occasional disputes, which will be discussed later, the nations around the North Sea continental shelf have achieved satisfactory division of the shelf among themselves. These agreements were reached, in general, through the application of the equidistance or median line as provided for in the Convention.

Mention should be made, however, of one exception to the equidistance method, namely the 1968 agreement between Iran and Saudi Arabia, under which a line between Iran and Saudi Arabia is to be drawn so as to divide equally all the exploitable oil resources in the theretofore disputed areas.[12] The line was actually drawn near the coast of Saudi Arabia in favour of Iran's claim. This was hardly a

TABLE 10. BILATERAL AGREEMENT ON BOUNDARIES OF THE CONTINENTAL SHELF

North Sea

U.K.* - Norway	10 Mar. 1965	(A)
U.K.* - Netherlands	6 Oct. 1965	(C)
U.K.* - Denmark *	3 Mar. 1966	(B)
Norway - Denmark *	8 Dec. 1965	(D)
Denmark * - Netherlands *	31 Mar. 1966	(G)
Germany - Netherlands	1 Dec. 1964	(F)
Germany - Denmark *	9 June 1965	(E)

Baltic Sea

U.S.S.R.* - Finland *	5 May 1967

Gulf of Finland

U.S.S.R.* - Finland *	20 May 1965

Adriatic Sea

Italy - Yugoslavia *	8 Jan. 1968

Persian Gulf

Iran - Saudi Arabia	24 Oct. 1968

(Asterisk indicates States ratifying the Continental Shelf Convention or acceding to it. A-G indicate the boundaries shown in Map 1.)

geographical median line, but it represented a solution based on the economic realities of equitable distribution of resources.

---

11. See Oda, S., "Boundary of the Continental Shelf", *Japanese Annual of International Law,* Vol. 12, 1968, pp. 264, 272.

12. *International Legal Materials,* Vol. 8, 1969, p. 493.

MAP 1

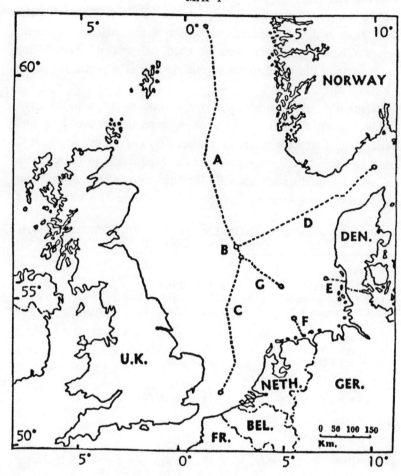

A-G indicate the boundaries of the continental shelf provided for in the
bilateral agreements shown in table 10.

92

(ii) Equidistance Line—Desirable or Not?

The question naturally arises of whether use of the equidistance or median line is actually desirable or advisable in drawing a boundary. Does this line necessarily provide the most reasonable solution in all cases? The fact is that situations and conditions in different parts of the world are too varied to permit a categorical adoption of the equidistance or median line as a rule for boundaries. The cases where the equidistance or median line offers an equitable solution are likely to occur infrequently and exceptions will probably be more numerous than the rule.

In 1951, the International Law Commission made no reference to any equidistance line. The only solutions proposed were by agreement or resort to compulsory arbitration *ex aequo et bono*. In the view of the International Law Commission in 1951, the boundary of the continental shelf, where the territories of two oppositely located States are separated by an arm of the sea, would generally coincide with some median line between the two coasts.[13] The case of two adjacent States was not even mentioned. In 1953, after considering the conclusions of the committee of experts on the technical problems of the territorial sea, the International Law Commission felt prepared to formulate a general rule based on the principle of equidistance which would apply to the boundaries of the continental shelf not only in case of States facing but also States adjoining each other.[14] The median line of the continental shelf may perhaps be acceptable where two States face each other, because, as a general rule, it would divide the continental shelf on a more or less equitable basis. But if the equidistance line for two adjacent States is to be reasonable, it must be made perpendicular to the common coastline. The analogy drawn in 1953 between the boundary of the territorial seas and the extended region of the continental shelf represented gross error. The boundary of the territorial seas between adjacent States, however inequitably drawn, would probably not materially affect the interests of the two States in sea resources, because in any event the territorial sea ends

---

13. *Report of the International Law Commission, 1951*, p. 19.
14. *Id., 1953*, p. 7 and p. 15 (iv).

relatively near the coast. Quite contrary is the case of an inequitably drawn boundary for the continental shelf, which generally extends far beyond the territorial sea.

(iii) Recommendations

The equidistance line certainly offers one practical solution, but only where the drawing of the line actually results in an equitable division of the continental shelf among the States concerned. The equidistance line, as such, hardly represents a general principle for determining boundaries of the continental shelf. It is merely a formula based upon the fundamental concept of equitable division, and it is successful only where an extremely simple geographic configuration exists. It would seem highly desirable to include in the Continental Shelf Convention a provision that, in determination of the boundary of the continental shelf between opposite as well as adjacent States, either by agreement or by an impartial third-party determination, the principle of equitable division of the continental shelf should control. Unlike a mechanical principle such as the equidistance line, the idea of equitable division of the continental shelf does not necessarily assure an automatic or easy solution, but it can provide a starting point for negotiation or resort to a third-party decision. Of course, where a State can convincingly cite special circumstances and persuade another State or a tribunal of their force, modification of the rule would be very much in order.

(iv) The North Sea Continental Shelf Cases

The dispute between Germany, on the one hand, and Denmark and the Netherlands, on the other, concerning the boundary of the continental shelf of the North Sea, points up the problem of adjacent States, and examination of the cases is illuminating in this respect.[15] Denmark, Germany and the Netherlands, which border the eastern portion of the North Sea, failed to reach agreement on the boundary of the continental shelf. Denmark and the Netherlands, whose territories are not adjacent, agreed on 31 March 1966, upon a

15. *I.C.J. Reports 1969, North Sea Continental Shelf Cases (Federal Republic of Germany/Denmark; Federal Republic of Germany/Netherlands),* 1969.

boundary line between the continental shelves of the two countries. This line starts from a point on the boundary line separating the United Kingdom's shelf from the eastern half of the North Sea and proceeds to a point off the coast of Germany. It thus prevents Germany from extending its own shelf-line to the middle of the North Sea where it might otherwise meet the United Kingdom's boundary line. In their agreement, Denmark and the Netherlands stated that this boundary rests on the application of the principle of the equidistance line. Germany, however, could ill afford to acquiesce in this view, since the German approach held that there is no such thing in customary international law as the "rule of the equidistance line".

On 2 February 1967, Special Agreements were concluded between Germany, on the one side, and Denmark and the Netherlands, on the other. The International Court of Justice was requested to determine the principles and rules of international law applicable to the delimitation among these nations in respect of the areas of the continental shelf in the North Sea. Germany had not ratified the Continental Shelf Convention and thus considered itself free to ignore the rule of the equidistance line provided for in the Convention. This was the issue in the matter placed before the International Court of Justice.

The Court, delivering its judgment on 20 February 1969, stated that the provisions of Article 6 of the Convention relating to the boundary of the continental shelf are not of the same norm-creating character as Articles 1 and 2, which deal with the fundamental features of the continental shelf regime, and that, therefore, they do not bind Germany, which had not ratified the Convention. In support of its conclusion, the Court made the following arguments: First, Article 6 is so framed as to give priority to the obligation to effect delimitation by agreement, and to place second the obligation to make use of the equidistance method. Second, the notion of special circumstances relative to the principle of equidistance as embodied in Article 6 raises further doubts as to the potentially norm-creating character of the rule. Third, the ease with which Article 6 may be qualified makes it all the more difficult to accept as a general proposition of law the so-called equidistance principle.

The Court states further that there is no single method of delimitation obligatory and satisfactory in all circumstances and that:

delimitation is to be effected by agreement in accordance with equitable principles, and taking account of all the relevant circumstances, in such a way as to leave as much as possible to each party all those parts of the continental shelf that constitute a natural prolongation of its land territory into and under the sea, without encroachment on the natural prolongation of the land territory of the other.[16]

The judgment then lists some of the factors which should be taken into account: (1) the general configuration of the coasts of the parties, as well as the presence of any special or unusual features; (2) the physical and geological structure and natural resources of the continental shelf areas involved; (3) the element of a reasonable degree of proportionality, which a delimitation ought to achieve between the extent of the continental shelf areas appertaining to the coastal State and the length of its coast measured in the general direction of the coastline.

(c) Existence of Islands

(i) An Example of the Gulf of Persia

The problem of drawing a boundary for the continental shelf among neighbouring States, either opposite or adjacent to each other, is further complicated by the existence of islands. The dispute over the Gulf of Persia is a prime example.[17] Saudi Arabia, Kuwait and Iran, which border the northern portion of the Gulf, have maintained that continental shelf boundaries with neighbouring countries should be drawn on principles of equity, and in this respect the three nations are fundamentally in accord on principle. However, concessions which have been granted by the respective countries tend to overlap each other in certain parts of the region, and this derives from differing notions of "equity", which in turn depend on how these States choose to deal with the question of islands.

(ii) Deliberations at the Geneva Conference

Article 1 of the Continental Shelf Convention provides that the continental shelf shall mean not only the submarine areas adjacent

---

16. *ICJ Reports 1969*, p. 53.
17. See Oda, S., *op. cit., supra,* note 11, p. 265.

to a continent but also those adjacent to the coasts of islands. This provision was suggested at the 1958 Geneva Conference by the delegate from the Philippines undoubtedly for the reason that the Philippines, an island nation, should have the same claim to the continental shelf as any continental country; and the suggestion is grounded in reason. But, to take every island into account in drawing the boundary of the continental shelf would lead to most unreasonable results. Because of this, the existence of islands was considered at the Geneva Conference simply as a special circumstance justifying deviation from the median line. This became clear from the Italian and the Iranian proposals, which recommended that, where islands exist on a contiguous continental shelf, the median line serving as a boundary should be drawn solely on the basis of coastlines, no consideration being given to the islands as islands.[18] The Iranian delegate felt that serious complications would arise if another approach were adopted and that the benefit of the median line rule would then disappear because of the very difficulty of applying it.

Referring to the presence of a small or large island in the area to be apportioned, Captain Kennedy, a member of the United Kingdom delegation, suggested that, for the purpose of delineating boundaries, islands should be treated as their size merited, very small islands or sand cays on a continuous continental shelf and outside the belts of territorial sea being quite properly ignored as base points for measurement.[19] The United States delegate agreed with the delegate from the United Kingdom that, because of the great variety of size, grouping and position of islands, it would be impossible as a general proposition either to include or to exclude all islands on the continental shelf, and that therefore each case should be considered on its merits.[20] Although the Italian and the Iranian proposals were rejected, it would be incorrect to conclude that consequently all islands on the continental shelf are to be considered in delimiting the boundary of the continental shelf.[21]

---

18. UN Doc. A/CONF. 13/C.4/L.25/Rev.1; A/CONF.13/C.4/L.60.
19. *UN Conference on the Law of the Sea, 1958,* Vol. VI, p. 93.
20. *Id.,* p. 95.
21. See Gutteridge, J. A. C., "The 1958 Geneva Convention on the Continental Shelf", *British Year Book of International Law,* Vol. 35, 1959, pp. 110, 120.

(iii) Recommendations

But a note of caution: a small island which is not now counted as a basis for delimiting the continental shelf among the States may one day become an independent nation and claim the continental shelf for its own. This may well lead to redistribution of the areas of the continental shelf which may be claimed by the various States adjacent to the shelf. If, however, as in most cases, the island is merely an elevation of the continental shelf, there is no reason to consider this land rise in delimiting the shelf. Of course, the size and location of a particular island, the degree of its exploitation, and its population may justify considering the island as a "special circumstance" to be taken into account in determining an equitable delimitation.

The Continental Shelf Convention should be revised to provide that only in such special cases should the existence of an island be a determinant in dividing up the continental shelf among the various nations.

A similarly vexatious problem will arise in the case of an island lying beyond the continental shelf of the nation to which it belongs. The solution of whether it can claim its continental shelf as its own will have to depend on the merits of the individual case.

5. Exploitation of the Continental Shelf and Other Legitimate Uses of the Superjacent High Seas

How can the exploitation and development of the continental shelf be reconciled with other uses of the high seas; and how can the exploitation of the continental shelf be geared to the regime of the sea as a whole? It should not be ignored that exploitation of the continental shelf, which is carried out mainly in the waters above the continental shelf, affects the legitimate uses of the superjacent high seas to a greater or lesser degree, depending on the intensity of use.

It is not an easy task to accommodate the often conflicting uses of the high seas. Navigation and fishing, both expressly protected under freedom of the high seas, may often run counter to each other. And the effect of exploitation on the water itself, as well as its inhabitants, will give rise to conflict. Under the Continental Shelf Convention, the

98

use of the continental shelf is circumscribed by the legitimate interests of other States on the high seas. The Convention provides:

Art. 5, para. 1—. . . the exploration of the continental shelf and the exploitation of its natural resources must not result in any unjustifiable interference with navigation, fishing or the conservation of the living resources of the sea . . .

What is "unjustifiable interference" with other legitimate uses as a result of the exploration of the continental shelf and the exploitation of its natural resources is subject to debate. However, the common interest in free navigation or fishing must be balanced against the exclusive interests of the coastal State to work the continental shelf resources.

While construction, maintenance and operation on the continental shelf of installations and other devices necessary for its exploration and the exploitation of its natural resources are undoubtedly permissible, due notice must be given of such impediments and permanent means for warning of their presence must be maintained. These installations or devices may not be established in locations where they may interfere with the use of recognised sea lanes essential to international navigation. Important also in this respect is the prevention of pollution of sea waters, which may occur with working of the continental shelf, through oil leakage or radioactivity from devices used in exploration or exploitation. Although the Continental Shelf Convention is faultily drafted in this connection, it does appear to obligate the coastal State, in case of the exploitation of the continental shelf, to undertake all appropriate measures for the protection of living resources of the sea from harmful agents.

6. Legal Status of the Superjacent Waters of the Continental Shelf

(a) Relevant Provisions of the Convention

In any consideration of the numerous uses of the waters above the continental shelf (navigation, fishing, the laying of submarine cables and pipelines, general exploitation of the waters' resources themselves, etc.) the vital question must be asked whether the coastal State controlling the continental shelf may have any control or authority over the superjacent waters. The short answer to this is "No".

The coastal State's title to the continental shelf does not impart to that State any power or authority with respect to fishing, navigation, etc., in the superjacent waters. These activities may be engaged in by other States as legitimate interests guaranteed under freedom of the high seas. Article 3 of the Continental Shelf Convention makes this clear:

Art. 3—The rights of the coastal State over the continental shelf do not affect the legal status of the superjacent waters as high seas, or that of the air space above those waters.

This idea was accepted as beyond dispute during the International Law Commission's deliberations. The Commission stated in its comments to the 1956 draft that "a claim to sovereign rights in the continental shelf can only extend to the seabed and subsoil and not to the superjacent waters", and that "the articles on the continental shelf are intended as laying down the regime of the continental shelf, only as subject to and within the orbit of the paramount principle of the freedom of the seas and of the airspace above them".[22] Although there was little discussion of this problem at the Geneva Conference, the provision referred to above was adopted overwhelmingly. Moreover, the International Court of Justice, in its judgment, gave Article 3 of the Continental Shelf Convention its imprimatur as a rule of customary international law. It appears *prima facie*, therefore, that the meaning and import of these provisions is not open to question.

(b) Inevitable Exercise of Coastal Authorities

Exclusive control over submarine areas by the coastal State will inevitably require some corresponding measure of control of the high sea areas above the continental shelf.[23] In this, the author espouses a decidedly minority view, but it seems naïve to expect that, once the regime of the continental shelf is accepted, the coastal State should still remain powerless to exercise its jurisdiction over foreign vessels on the superjacent waters. Logic mandates, for example, that the coastal State should be empowered to exercise jurisdiction over

---

22. *Report of the International Law Commission, 1956*, p. 43.
23. This view has been repeatedly stated by the author. See Oda, S., *International Control of Sea Resources*, 1963, p. 168.

foreign drilling vessels which have encroached upon the superjacent waters of its continental shelf or which have begun to exploit its continental shelf. The argument that this area above the continental shelf is a part of the high seas should not be used to deprive the coastal State of its right. Any other approach would be extremely unrealistic in the light of the entire regime of the continental shelf.

Inherent in the adoption of the concept of the continental shelf is an inevitable modification of the entire concept of freedom of the superjacent high seas, a modification requiring the exercise of coastal-State jurisdiction in order to control exploration of the continental shelf and exploitation of its resources. Reason requires that the coastal State be competent to prevent intrusion on the waters superjacent to the continental shelf by foreign vessels seeking to explore the continental shelf or to exploit its resources without first securing the permission of the coastal State. Similarly, coastal States should be able to prevent foreign vessels from violating their regulations on exploration or exploitation and to punish violators.

In this respect, the superjacent waters of the continental shelf should, to some extent, be accorded a status similar to that of the contiguous zone seas. Naturally, just as in the contiguous zone, the exercise of control or power or the assertion of jurisdiction by the coastal State in the superjacent waters should not interfere with the legitimate exercise of such activities as fishing or navigation and should be limited to protection of the legitimate interests of the coastal State without affecting the legitimate interests of others. This concept should be explicitly set forth in the Convention.

(c) Installations and their Surrounding Safety Zones

The exploration and especially the exploitation of the continental shelf resources are mainly conducted from installations or devices constructed in the superjacent high sea areas. There is no question that the criminal and civil laws of the coastal State are applicable to any act of commission or omission which occurs on an installation, and that the coastal State has full jurisdiction in this case, as it has on a ship of its flag.[24]

24. See the United Kingdom's Continental Shelf Act, 1964 (1964, Chap. 29), art. 3. *International Law Materials*, Vol. 3, 1964, p. 564. Cf. Samuels, A.,

101

There is thus a present need for a regulation of the legal status of such installations and their surrounding safety zones. Under the Continental Shelf Convention, a safety zone may be established around installations for a distance of 500 metres, and within this zone, the coastal State is entitled to take measures necessary for the protection of installations. Ships of all nationalities must respect this safety zone (Art. 5, paras. 2 and 3). The object and character of the safety zone were not discussed at any length at the Geneva Conference, although Dr. Mouton, a well-known specialist on the continental shelf, advanced the argument, in his capacity as the delegate of the Netherlands, that the zone should be a "protective no-fire" area extending for 50 metres around installations, and augmented his proposal with certain reliable data obtained from oil companies.[25] The Conference, however, adopted the 500-metre zone proposed by the delegate from Yugoslavia, but the intention of those who drafted the Convention is not altogether clear, so far as the status of the safety zone is concerned.

If the safety zone is for the purpose of fire protection, 50 metres, as suggested by the oil companies, would be sufficient. Thus, something more than fire protection must have been contemplated when the safety zone of 500 metres was established. Do the permissible measures taken by the coastal State include prohibiting foreign vessels from entering the zone, or from anchoring or trawling in the zone? Do the designation of navigation routes and the limitation of the kind and size of vessels passing through the safety zone fall within the purview of these measures? In the event foreign vessels strike against the installations, does the coastal State have a right to seize the offending vessel in the safety zone? If this is the case, precisely what powers and competence the coastal State can exercise in the zone should be made clear. Neither the debates at the 1958 Geneva Conference nor the provisions of the Continental Shelf Convention provide any real answers to these questions.

If measures are really needed for the protection and safety of the installations or devices, it should follow that the coastal State is

---

"The Continental Shelf Act, 1964", *Developments in the Law of the Sea 1958-1964*, p. 155.
25. UN Doc. A/CONF. 13/C.4/L.22.

entitled to enforce its rules as against any foreign vessels entering the safety zone. A case can certainly be made out for giving the coastal State the power to enact regulations applicable to the zone for the purpose of protecting the installations and punishing violaters. However, if such regulations were to affect navigation or fishing adversely, they would again raise the problem of the conflict between the interest of the coastal State in the continental shelf and the interest of other States in the use of the high seas. This is not merely a problem of the safety zone but one that goes to the heart of the regime of the continental shelf, i.e., the exclusive use of the continental shelf by the coastal State.

SUPPLEMENT TO CHAPTER IV

1. Boundaries of the Continental Shelf

The author, who was critical of the provisions of the Continental Shelf Convention relevant to the boundaries of the continental shelf, suggested ten years ago (page 94) that they should be revised, taking the concept of equity into consideration. He is now quite satisfied to see that the relevant provision of the Informal Composite Negotiating Text[1] (Article 83-1) has been properly drafted along the lines he had proposed. In other words, equity is suggested in the Text as the basic principle to be followed in determining the boundaries, and the median or equidistance line should be employed only where appropriate, taking into account all the relevant circumstances.

Since the 1969 judgment of the International Court of Justice a fair number of bilateral treaties have been concluded on the delimitation of the boundary of the continental shelf of the North Sea, the Persian Gulf and the Indian Ocean and in South-East Asia.[2] A recent example is also found in the conclusion of a boundary agreement in 1974 between Japan and the Republic of Korea.[3] The majority of these cases concern the drawing of boundaries between States, the respective coasts of those States being opposite to each other. The principles which were applied to the determination of the boundary lines varied according to each case, but, it can be said that equity which is reflected in most cases in the median line is a principle observed in these treaties.

The author suggested, however, that the idea of equity would not be an automatic or easy solution, but that it could provide a starting point for negotiation or recourse to a third-party decision. He then predicted that the existence of small islands would inevitably cause great difficulties in applying the concept of equity (page 98). This prediction has become a reality. One of the most outstanding cases with regard to the status of islands concerns the Aegean Sea, the highly complicated geographical and geological features of which have caused political and legal difficulties among the nations in this region. These difficulties have given rise to extensive exchanges of views in the United Nations Seabed Committee and the Third Law of the Sea Conference over the problem of delimiting boundaries in connection with off-shore areas rich in resources. In the 1973 sessions of the Seabed Committee, Turkey and Greece submitted in turn proposals to strengthen their respective positions in this area. Turkey suggested that, where the coasts of two or

---

1. UN Doc. A/CONF.62/WP.10 and Add. 1.
2. See Oda,*The International Law of the Ocean Development,* Part VII.
3. See Oda, *The Law of the Sea in Our Time – I: New Developments 1966-1975,* pp. 249-265.

more States are adjacent or opposite to each other, the respective maritime boundaries should be determined by agreement, taking into account all the relevant circumstances including special circumstances such as the configuration of the coasts, the existence of islands of another State and the physical and geological structure of the marine area involved. On the other hand, Greece proposed that the provisions applicable to the determination of the "continental shelf" and the "zones of national jurisdiction" of the continental part of the State should apply, in principle, to islands.

Also, in a more general manner, the status of islands in the delimitation of the sea boundary has become a subject of extensive discussions of the Seabed Committee. A suggestion to take into account the existence of islands depending on their own merits was made. In draft articles submitted by fourteen African nations with regard to the economic zone in the 1973 Spring Session, (a) the size of islands; (b) population; (c) their contiguity to the principal territory; (d) whether or not they are situated on the continental shelf of another territory; (e) their geological and geomorphological structure and configuration, were all suggested as relevant factors in determining the maritime space.[4] A draft article submitted by four African nations (Cameroon, Kenya, Madagascar and Tunisia), together with Turkey, singled out the above-mentioned proposal of the fourteen African nations' draft articles.[5] Romania also presented a working paper to suggest that islets and small islands, uninhabited and without economic life, which are situated on the continental shelf of the coast, do not possess any aspects of the "continental shelf" or other marine space of the same nature.[6] Romania also suggested that such islands may have waters, the extent of which should be determined by agreement, but the waters thus determined should not in any event affect marine spaces which belong to the State or to neighbouring States.

The difficult situations concerning the delimitation of the maritime jurisdiction zones were brought before the Law of the Sea Conference. The confrontation among the nations surrounding the Aegean Sea has become more furious, as is reflected in the alternate submissions of proposals and counter-proposals by Turkey and Greece. The Greek position was strengthened by some other island nations, when Fiji, New Zealand, Tonga and Western Samoa suggested that "the economic zone of an island and its continental shelf are determined in accordance with the provisions of this Convention applicable to other land territory".[7] On the other hand, Ireland revised its previous position so as to state that "in determining a median line account may be taken of an island, only if it is inhabited and if (i) it is situated less than the breadth of the

---

4. UN Doc. A/AC.138/SC.II/L.40.
5. UN Doc. A/AC.138/SC.II/L.43.
6. UN Doc. A/AC.138/SC.II/L.53.
7. UN Doc. A/CONF.62/C.2/L.30.

territorial sea from the coast or (ii) it contains at least one-tenth of the land area and population of the State concerned".[8]

The Informal Composite Negotiating Text is silent on the status of islands in drawing the boundary of the continental shelf. The only provisions relevant to the status of islands are simply borrowed from the Greek concept and they read, in Article 121-2: "the territorial sea, the contiguous zone, the exclusive economic zone and the continental shelf of an island are determined in accordance with the provisions of the present Convention applicable to other land territory". Without giving any evaluation of either position, the author submits that the relevant provisions of the Text which do not or cannot provide any solution to these complicated contemporary problems do not seem to lessen the existing confusion with regard to a question of islands, which requires some guiding principles in order to arrive at a satisfactory solution.

2. Parallelism between the Exclusive Economic Zone and the Continental Shelf

The two separate regimes of the exclusive economic zone and the continental shelf are proposed in parallel in the Informal Composite Negotiating Text. The first question which springs to mind is whether the seabed within 200-miles from the coast should be incorporated in the regime of the exclusive economic zone or whether it should come under a separate regime of the continental shelf. The parallelism does not, however, seem to fit in with the very idea of the exclusive economic zone, which suggests that the coastal State should possess "sovereign rights for the purpose of exploring and exploiting ... the natural resources, whether living or non-living, of the seabed and subsoil and the superjacent waters" (Article 56-1(a)). Do the rights of the coastal State to mineral resources within the 200-mile zone require further guarantees to be specifically spelled out under a separate regime of the continental shelf? Certainly the rights of the coastal State over the exploitation of living resources within its exclusive economic zone are more restricted in order to give some specified nations such as land-locked States or States with special geographical characteristics access to those living resources which the coastal State cannot itself exploit. However, this does not seem necessarily to justify the existence of two separate regimes of the continental shelf and the exclusive economic zone which apply either to the seabed or to superjacent waters. If the regime of the continental shelf is to have any meaning at all under the new law of the sea, this seems simply to come, on the one hand, from the fact that, while the concept of exclusive economic zones is new, the regime of the continental shelf is deemed to have already secured its establishment in the 1960s, and, on the other hand, from the necessity of placing the seabed

---

8. UN Doc. A/CONF.62/C.2/L.43.

area beyond the 200-mile limit, but within the outer edge of the continental margin, under the exclusive control of the coastal State.

The parallelism between the exclusive economic zone and the continental shelf will inevitably meet further difficulties in connection with the division of maritime jurisdiction between neighbouring, either adjacent or opposite, States. A question which may be asked is whether it is legitimate to suggest two separate regimes for the same offshore areas, i.e., the economic zone for the superjacent waters and the continental shelf for the seabed, as a result of drawing separate boundaries for each between the same neighbouring countries. Is it permissible to have the seabed as part of the continental shelf of one State while the superjacent waters above it are under the jurisdiction of the other State as part of the latter's economic zone? It is noteworthy that in the Informal Composite Negotiating Text the provisions concerning delimitation between adjacent or opposite States for both the exclusive economic zone and the continental shelf are practically identical, except that the definition of "median or equidistance line" is provided for only in the case of the exclusive economic zone. Both provisions contain a phrase to the effect that where there is an agreement in force between the States concerned, questions relating to the delimitation of the exclusive economic zone or the continental shelf shall be determined in accordance with the provisions of that agreement. It is likely that the agreements in force may be separate depending upon the exclusive economic zone or the continental shelf. After all, it looks as though the Text anticipates quite separate lines of determination for the seabed and the superjacent waters. Is this conclusion really compatible with the idea of the exclusive economic zone as suggested? If the coastal State has sovereign rights for the purpose of exploiting the mineral resources of any specific area of the seabed within its 200-mile exclusive economic zone, how can this area be a part of the continental shelf of a neighbouring State?

If, on the other hand, the boundaries of the continental shelf on the seabed and the exclusive economic zone in the superjacent waters are to be parallel, further queries may be raised. Firstly, does the boundary of the continental shelf have priority over the boundary of the exclusive economic zone on the ground that its regime came into being first? But is it legitimate to say that the lateral boundary which could have been drawn on the seabed in the 1960s by the neighbouring adjacent States extended to 200 miles from the coast (the newly suggested outer limit of the continental shelf), far beyond the 200-metre isobath (considered in the 1960s as the outer limit of the continental shelf)? Considering the case of opposite States, on the other hand, is it legitimate to say that the outer limit of the continental shelf of any State in the 1960s extended to a distance of 200 miles from the coast, jumping over deep troughs or trenches near the coast of that State? Secondly, the principles of equity as the Text suggests shall be taken into account in negotiations between the neighbouring States for drawing the boundaries in the case both of the continental shelf and of the exclusive economic zone. But the factors to be taken into account in considering what is equitable with regard to the delimitation of the superjacent waters may not always be the same as those in the case of the seabed boundary. Is it legitimate to say that in any future negotiations among the States concerned, the principles of equity applicable in the case of the seabed should always claim priority over those which may apply to the delimitation of the boundaries of the exclusive economic zone? No answer to these questions can be found in the provisions of the Text. Considering the great competence exercised by the coastal State either in the 200-mile exclusive economic zone or on the continental shelf, and expecting untapped treasures of the sea and the seabed in these zones, most nations are now biassed by their own geographical and geological conditions in their presentation of the issues concerning maritime boundaries. There is still a long way to go before any satisfactory agreement on these issues can be reached.

CHAPTER V

REGIME OF THE DEEP OCEAN FLOOR

1. Historical Backgrounds

(a) Progress of Work in the United Nations

A few short years ago, there was little hint that so many governmental figures, international lawyers, scientists and others would soon become excited by the prospect of the vast benefits to be derived from the last frontiers of the earth, the deep ocean floor. Yet today we are literally flooded with suggestions, proposals, recommendations, and draft conventions, prepared by non-governmental organisations and private individuals, on the use of the deep ocean floor.[1]

Ambassador Pardo, permanent representative of Malta to the United Nations, first drew the attention of the world to this vast untapped area, the resources of which, according to him, would tax the imagination. At the 22nd session of the United Nations General Assembly in 1967, Ambassador Pardo pointed out four distinct problems: (1) non-appropriation of the deep ocean floor by any State; (2) exploration of this area in accordance with the principles and objectives of the United Nations Charter; (3) use of this area for the benefit of mankind, the economic benefit therefrom being especially utilised for the development of the poorer nations; (4) exclusive reservation of this area for peaceful purposes.[2]

On 18 December 1967 the United Nations General Assembly unanimously passed a resolution (General Assembly Resolution 2340 (XXII)) on "Examination of the question of the reservation exclu-

---

1. E.g., Borgese, E. M., *The Ocean Regime,* California, 1968; World Peace Through Law Center (United Nations Committee), *Treaty Governing the Exploration and Use of the Ocean Bed,* 1968; US Senator C. Pell, *Proposed Ocean Space Treaty,* 5 March 1968.
2. UN Doc. A/6695: *Note Verbale dated 17 August 1967 from the Permanent Mission of Malta to the United Nations addressed to the Secretary-General.*

sively for peaceful purposes of the seabed and the ocean floor, and the subsoil thereof, underlying the high seas beyond the limits of present national jurisdiction, and the use of their resources in the interests of mankind". An *ad hoc* committee consisting of 35 States was charged with the task of preparing a study, which was also to provide practical guidelines for promoting international co-operation in the exploration and use of the deep ocean floor and the conservation of its resources. This committee, after three sessions in 1968, issued its report but failed to agree on a single set of legal principles which would govern the use of this area.[3] In the course of their deliberations it became clear that the interests represented by the diverse groups at the table, developing countries and developed countries, capitalist countries and socialist countries, were too far apart for achieving a compromise solution within the limited time.

At its 23rd session the United Nations General Assembly adopted another resolution (General Assembly Resolution 2467A (XXIII): 21 December 1968) on the same subject, establishing a standing committee of 42 States. The objective of this committee is to develop legal principles and norms to promote international co-operation in the exploration and use of the deep ocean floor and to ensure the proper exploitation of its resources for the benefit of mankind. This 42-nation committee, after three sessions in 1969, prepared a report for the consideration of the General Assembly, which report, however, does not exhaust the problems assigned to the Committee.[4]

(b) Two Distinct Areas for Two Different Objectives

In treating the regime of the deep ocean floor, the United Nations seems to have erred by lumping together the question of the military or non-military uses of the seabed with the problem of exploration and exploitation of the resources of the area. In connection with exclusive reservation of subsea areas "for peaceful purposes", it should be pointed out that the areas "beyond the limits of present national jurisdiction" are those beneath the high seas *beyond the territorial seas*. The continental shelf is the area over which the coastal

---

3. UN Doc. A/7230.
4. UN Doc. A/7622.

State has rights only for the purposes of exploration and exploitation of natural resources; military or non-military use of the seabed is quite irrelevant to the regime of the continental shelf. On the other hand, the natural resources which should be utilised "in the interests of mankind" are undoubtedly those existing in the areas *beyond the continental shelf*, which generally extends far beyond the limits of the territorial sea.

It is thus clear that the areas "beyond the limits of present national jurisdiction" with which the United Nations General Assembly in its resolutions of 1967 and 1968 attempted to deal, are intended to refer to two distinct areas and two different objectives: the areas beyond the territorial sea for exclusive reservation for peaceful purposes, on the one hand, and the areas beyond the continental shelf for the use of resources in the interests of mankind, on the other. The problem of the peaceful uses of the seabed is too important to admit of confusion, although in the course of their deliberations in 1968 and 1969, the United Nations committee on peaceful uses of the seabed apparently overlooked the distinction between exclusive reservation for peaceful purposes and use of resources in the interests of mankind.

The increasingly significant questions underlying the military and peaceful uses of the seabed should be viewed in the context of the use of the ocean as a whole, without being limited to the seabed alone or to the area beyond the continental shelf. To turn from this problem to that of the commercial utilisation of the seabed beyond national jurisdiction, there are two questions which must be examined in connection with the regime of the deep ocean floor: first, what area of the seabed should be considered "deep ocean floor" under the cognisance of the United Nations committee; and second, what should be the regime of and the principles for that area?

2. Areas Beyond the Continental Shelf

(a) Diverse Proposals for Outer Limit of the Continental Shelf

The deep ocean floor begins where the continental shelf ends. As explained previously, the outer limit of the continental shelf is one of the most hotly debated points of the Continental Shelf Convention.

111

The interpretation of the relevant provision of the Convention will play a large role in shaping future policy.

Whatever the outer limit of the continental shelf may eventually be, there seems to be widespread agreement that the shelf should not be extended indefinitely and that precise boundaries can and should be fixed for the deep ocean floor. Conversely, from time to time recommendations have been made with emphasis on the outer limit of the continental shelf, in other words, the inner limit of the deep ocean floor.

As early as the Geneva Conference of 1958, the delegate from the Netherlands thought that it might be advisable to specify a depth line of 550 metres as being nearer to the deepest edge of the continental shelf,[5] while the delegates of Norway and the United Arab Republic proposed a limitation of the continental shelf based upon distance from the coast.[6]

Some delegates to the 1968 *ad hoc* committee on the peaceful uses of the seabed and to the standing committee on the same subject in 1969 proposed delimiting the continental shelf in terms of distance from the coast, or at least granting to each State the right to choose more advantageous criteria, either of the depth of the waters or of the distance from the coast ranging from 40 to 60 miles. And in 1968, the delegate of Norway suggested a combination of either 500 or 600 metres depth for superjacent waters and 200 miles distance from the coast.[7] Certain Latin American States feel that, since the 200-mile limit from the coast has already been provided for in their own Constitutions, their nations should not be prejudiced by considerations contradictory to these Constitutions.

In the drafts prepared by non-governmental bodies, moreover, there is wide divergence of opinion on the proposed limits of the continental shelf. Recommendations of private groups may be summarised as follows:

(i) Retention of the 200-metre isobath approach: According to this approach, the "exploitability" clause should simply be omitted from the Continental Shelf Convention.

---

5. *UN Conference on the Law of the Sea, 1958,* Vol. VI, p. 6.
6. *Id.,* pp. 5, 27.
7. UN Doc. A/AC.135/WG.1/SR.6, p. 39.

(ii) Limits in terms of greater depth of the superjacent waters: Depth greater than 200 metres is recommended as a criterion for delimiting the continental shelf. The "exploitability" clause should be eliminated. For example, the 500-metre or the 600-metre isobath is suggested frequently. It may be recalled that these figures were discussed at the 1958 Geneva Conference.

(iii) Combination of the 200-metre or greater isobath and distance from the coast: Delimitation of the continental shelf through the criterion of depth alone would be inequitable to such countries as Chile, Peru and Ecuador, all on the western coast of South America, where the coast suddenly drops to great depth. For this reason, moves have been made to introduce a concept of distance from the coast, ranging generally between 40 and 60 miles.

(iv) Limits in terms of the geological structure of off-shore submarine areas: This method is strongly advanced by oil interests in the United States, which favour extension of the United States continental shelf seaward to the limit of the continental land mass, including the continental slope and continental rise. The American Bar Association and the American Branch of the International Law Association made almost identical proposals in 1968, suggesting that the submerged portions of the continental land mass be included in the legal definition of the continental shelf.[8] In the proposal of the latter group concrete figures are given: a tentative depth of 2,500 metres, and, alternatively, a distance of 100 miles from the coast. The National Petroleum Council, an industry advisory body to the Secretary of the Interior of the United States, representing the American oil and gas industries, in 1968 advised that, as a result of the interpretation of the "exploitability" clause of the Geneva Convention, the United States already possessed exclusive jurisdiction over the natural resources of the submerged continental mass seaward to where the submerged portion of that mass meets the abyssal ocean floor.[9] The Council, calling any

---

8. American Bar Association, *Joint Report of Sections of Natural Resources Law, International and Comparative Law, and the Standing Committee on Peace and Law through United Nations,* August 1968, pp. 11-12; American Branch of the International Law Association, Committee on Deep Sea Mineral Resources, *Interim Report,* 19 July 1968, p. XVII.
9. National Petroleum Council, *Petroleum Resources under the Ocean Floor,* March 1969, pp. 70-72. See *Interim Report,* 9 July 1968, pp. 9-10.

recommendation which would contradict this interpretation a "retro-active" boundary proposal, claimed that such a recommendation would reduce the national jurisdiction already granted to the United States under the Continental Shelf Convention.

(b) Policy Considerations on the Extent of the Continental Shelf

There is no doubt that the continental shelf is an area over which the coastal State has sovereign rights of exploration and exploitation. The debates as to how far the continental shelf should extend are closely related to policy considerations of how far each coastal State is entitled to monopolise off-shore submarine resources to the exclusion of other nations. Fundamentally, there are only two alternatives. One is that each coastal State is free to reserve to itself wider areas under the regime of the continental shelf, thus reducing the area beyond, namely the deep ocean floor. The other is to keep exclusive continental shelf areas of the coastal State as narrow as possible, if not narrower than the 200-metre isobath, and thus to ensure that the largest amount of resources found beyond that limit will be free from exclusive control of coastal States.

If only in its national interest, each State is naturally inclined to favour a wider extension of its own continental shelf. This is true not only for the developed States with advanced skills and adequate capital, but also for the developing countries, which are free to grant concessions to any advanced enterprises, thus receiving great benefit from their own widely extended areas of the continental shelf. Opposition to greater extension of the continental shelf originates in the principled desire to ensure that as many resources of the ocean floor will be available for mankind as a whole, thus guaranteeing equitable treatment for those geographically handicapped nations which are land-locked countries or which have only short coastlines or a narrow geologic continental shelf. Thus two motives exist for the recommendations of a narrower continental shelf limit. One is extremely idealistic and perhaps somewhat utopian in that it emphasises the concept of benefit to all mankind; while the other may be deemed more realistic, since it is concerned with the immediate interests of geographically handicapped nations, whose principal interest is the

114

internationalisation of as wide and extent of the ocean floor as possible for their own benefit.

Opposition to a wider extension of the continental shelf also comes from some of the more advanced States, which would stand to lose potential benefits existing off the coasts of other nations should such other nations claim a wider region to be under their own jurisdiction.

Thus, the line between the outer limits of the continental shelf and the inner limits of the deep ocean floor will, in the last analysis, depend entirely on the regime which will come to govern the latter area.

3. Regime of the Deep Ocean Floor

(a) Use of this Area for the Benefit of Mankind

Whatever line may separate the continental shelf from the deep ocean floor, the regime applicable to the latter should differ from the regime of the continental shelf. That is to say, the significance of a new regime for the deep ocean floor will be in the fact that the common interest in the area will be preserved, in contrast to the narrower interest of the coastal State, as in the case of the continental shelf.

The general consensus among the nations of the United Nations is that the deep ocean floor should be utilised for the benefit of mankind. In a resolution passed in 1967, the United Nations General Assembly stated that the exploration and use of this area should be "for the benefit of all mankind". Another resolution adopted the following year on the same subject mentions the exploitation of the resources of this area "for the benefit of mankind as a whole, irrespective of the geographical location of States, taking into account the special interests and needs of the developing countries". This principle has never been challenged by any nation in the forum of the United Nations. Former United States President Johnson declared that "we must ensure that the deep seas and the ocean bottoms are, and remain, the legacy of all human beings".[10] The term "common heritage of mankind" is often used in the United Nations as well as in

---

10. Statement by former President Johnson of the United States on 13 July 1966 at the commissioning of the new research ship "Oceanographer".

some private drafts to designate the general status of the deep ocean floor or to qualify the exploitation of its resources.

The concept of benefit to mankind is so vague, however, that it is extremely difficult to derive from it any clear-cut regime for the deep ocean floor, although it does see to set forth an unchallengeable principle that no part of the deep ocean floor should be appropriated by any State. Thus, no State may claim or exercise sovereign rights over any part of this area, nor may any part of the area be subjected to national appropriation by a claim of sovereignty, by use or occupation, or by any other means. The principle of non-appropriation of the deep ocean floor does not necessarily lead to the conclusion that exploration and exploitation of this area should come to a halt. On the contrary, in order to benefit mankind, the effective exploitation of the resources should be encouraged, and the incentives for this should not be removed. Free access to the resources of the deep ocean floor should be the right of all nations, not merely those possessing advanced technologies. Under the present rules of international law, the possibility still exists of free competition in the exploitation of the resources of the deep ocean floor.

(b) Who Is Entitled to Exploit the Resources of the Deep Ocean Floor?

(i) Two Alternatives

While free access to the deep ocean floor is guaranteed to all the nations under existing rules of international law *(lex lata), lex ferenda* provides alternate approaches to the problem: (1) free exploitation without restriction except the control of the flag State, this being the traditional system (laisser-faire system); and (2) exploitation under international control (international control system). To put it in different terms exploration and exploitation should be carried out either under the jurisdiction of the flag State, as in the case of high-seas fishing, or under international control, which would guarantee the orderly exploitation of ocean resources.

Two arguments support the mechanism of international control: (1) the strong demand of the more advanced nations and advanced enterprises, which look for certain assurances that the ocean floor

116

activities will be protected, and (2) the national interest of less developed and land-locked nations, which would otherwise derive little or no benefit from exploitation of the ocean floor.

To elaborate: the exploitation of the resources of the deep ocean floor, unlike high-seas fishing, requires substantial capital outlays which investors will quite understandably seek to secure in the best way possible. Under the principle of laisser-faire the discovery of any promising deposit will inevitably invite competition in its mining or working, and the resultant rivalry among enterprises could prove wasteful if not harmful. The advanced nations therefore seem to favour some kind of international regulation.

(ii) Functions of International Machinery—From Registration to Licence-Issuing: Interests of the Advanced Nations and Enterprises [11]

Mention is often made by the peoples of the advanced nations or enterprises of the necessity to create an international registry with which any project of exploration of the deep ocean floor or its exploitation would be registered, so that all the world might be informed of what is happening in connection with the exploration and exploitation of the deep ocean floor. This agency would have no regulatory power but would be simply a clearing-house for registration by each nation or enterprise undertaking exploration and exploitation.

In connection with the idea of an international registration system the first question which arises is, who is authorised to register its exploration or exploitation. There is a good deal of sentiment for the proposition that only a nation or an association of nations should be eligible to register and that whether the entity undertaking the actual exploration or exploitation may or may not be a national of the registering nation should be a matter for each nation to decide for itself. But there is no reason why a nation only, and not an enterprise, should be eligible to register.

---

11. See UN Doc. A/AC.138/12 and Corr. 1 and Add. 1 and Add. 1/Corr. 1 (incorporated in A/7622): Study on the Question of Establishing in Due Time Appropriate International Machinery for the Promotion of the Exploration and Exploitation of the Resources of the Sea-Bed and the Ocean Floor Beyond the Limits of National Jurisdiction, and the Use of these Resources in the Interests of Mankind (Report of the Secretary-General).

Under a registration system, it would be possible to observe the principle of "first come, first served", subject only to fulfilment of certain technical requirements such as financial or technical competence. The international registry authority would not be an organisation which would grant permission to explore or to exploit but would remain primarily a body with which a claim is registered. While the registrant with the international authority may not exercise sovereign rights over the area, the State of the flag of the registrant would unquestionably be competent to exercise its jurisdiction over a registrant carrying out exploration or exploitation in accordance with the conditions imposed by registration. This kind of jurisdiction would be exactly the same as that imposed upon vessels engaged in fishing on the high seas.

But what is the effect of registration? If an international registry functions merely as a clearing-house, competition among States or enterprises will still not be avoided. Registration should confer upon the registrant, either nation or individual, the exclusive right of exploitation in the affected area for a specified period of time. Without such a guarantee of the exclusivity or the priority of title to the right of exploration, registration would be meaningless.

The registration system is the most advantageous to States with advanced technologies and sufficient capital to enable them to undertake exploration or exploitation of the resources of the deep ocean floor, their claim being secured by registration which prevents unreasonable competition and possible conflict. This approach certainly conforms to the principle of using the resources of the deep ocean floor for the benefit of mankind, in the sense that everyone would be free to register upon the satisfaction of certain technical requirements. On the other hand, it is not likely that the developing nations would benefit from this approach, since the right to register with the international registry authority would still not guarantee their chance to participate in the exploration and exploitation of the deep ocean floor.

There is a strong feeling among many nations and commentators that, if an international organisation is established to control the use of the deep ocean floor, it should be given regulatory or licence-issuing authority. Such an organisation would certainly possess a more impressive competence than an international registration authority, since

118

exploration and exploitation of the deep ocean floor would be permitted only upon the grant of a licence or concession by this international body. The regulatory agency would be an extremely powerful body, in view of its discretion to determine the recipient of a licence or concession to initiate or to carry out exploration and exploitation and also to withhold or to revoke licences in the event that certain conditions are not met or fulfilled.

How would this authority be structured? What would its composition be? These are very difficult and complex questions which must be answered. Any international authority established to regulate the granting of licences or concessions will be required to observe or to develop criteria to be followed in making the grants. Should the rule of "first come, first served" be observed? Merely to state that the resources of the deep ocean floor should be developed for the benefit and in the interest of all mankind does not establish valid criteria for allocation of licences or concessions.

(c) Problems of Sharing Profits Derived from Exploitation: Interests of Developing Nations

Whether under the simpler registration system or under the more effective licencing system, the reality is that only the most advanced nations will stand to benefit, since the less developed countries will be hard put to it to undertake any significant exploration, let alone exploitation, of the deep ocean floor. It is natural, at least on the part of the latter, to claim a share of the profits derived from the exploitation undertaken by advanced nations or well-capitalised enterprises. In the view of the developing nations, their claims are justifiable under the concept that resources are the common heritage of mankind and should be utilised for the benefit of mankind.

It could be argued that such terms as "common heritage of mankind" and "benefit of mankind" mean only a guarantee to all nations of free access to resources. Under this view, the developing nations, which contribute little to the development of the resources of the deep ocean floor, can hardly expect to claim a share of benefits brought about by the costly undertakings of the advanced nations and enterprises simply because the area in question is situated beyond national jurisdiction. However, no body should ignore the growing demands of the developing countries for the benefits derived from exploitation of the deep ocean floor. In the view of these countries, the licensing authority should have the additional function of collecting royalties and fees for granting the right of exclusive exploration and exploitation and these revenues should be distributed among the developing nations.

It has become obvious to the advanced enterprises that it is impractical—and impracticable—for the advanced nations to ignore the growing claims of the developing countries to at least some of the benefits to be derived from this area. So long as incentive to provide the investment necessary for exploration and exploitation is not destroyed, the advanced States must come to grips with the necessity of offering some benefits to developing countries without obtaining any direct benefits in return.

At the second session of the United Nations *ad hoc* committee on the sea bed in June 1968, the following thought was put forward by the United States: it considered "as feasible and practicable" the "[d]edication . . . of a portion of the value of the resources recovered from the deep ocean floor to international community purposes".[12] It would be only prudent for the advanced nations to secure for themselves the benefits of exploration and exploitation of the resources of the deep ocean floor and to offer to the developing nations a portion of these benefits. Claimant enterprises would undoubtedly be prepared to dedicate some of the fruits of their exploration and exploitation if their rights of exploration and exploitation were protected through concessions or licences. This relinquishment would not be likely to reduce their incentive to make sizable capital investments.

A further question is raised as to how the revenues collected by the international licence-issuing authority through the grant of licences or concessions should be distributed. It has been suggested that these revenues be spent to solve the financial crisis of the United Nations. This suggestion, however, failed to secure a majority; and the use of these revenues for the benefit mainly of the developing nations is now being strongly advocated. It is thus clear that the concept of special

---

12. UN Doc. A/AC.135/25.

interests of developing nations in this respect is no longer being challenged. Moreover, the interests of land-locked countries are also being given special consideration. It is extremely difficult, however, to devise a generally acceptable formula for the distribution of benefits; and it might well be that, e.g., the UNDP or the World Bank could function as an international authority competent to distribute the profits realsed from this ocean-floor development.

To make the concept of allocation of revenues more palatable to geographically-handicapped developing nations, the creation of a buffer zone has been suggested by some non-governmental organisations in the United States. The idea is traceable to the American Assembly of 1968 and is fully explicated in the Report of the Commission on Marine Science, Engineering and Resources of 1969. The Commission recommends that:

> ... intermediate zones be created ... only to the 2,500-metre isobath, or 100 nautical miles, ... whichever alternative gives the coastal nation the greater area ... Only the coastal nation or its licensees, which may or may not be its nationals, should be authorized to explore or exploit the mineral resources of the intermediate zone. In all other respects, exploration and exploitation in the intermediate zone should be governed by the framework recommended above for the areas of the deep seas beyond the intermediate zone.[13]

If this suggestion is understood correctly, the coastal State only would have the exclusive right to control the exploitation of the intermediate zone, a situation comparable to the exploitation of its continental shelf, but—and here the parallel with the continental shelf ends—a portion of the profits derived from the exploitation of this intermediate zone would be sequestered for the benefit of the international community. It appears that a compromise lying somewhere between the exclusive interest of each coastal State and the community interest for the benefit of all finds proper expression in this concept of an intermediate or buffer zone.

---

13. *Our Nation and the Sea: Report of the Commission on Marine Science, Engineering and Resources,* 1969, p. 151.

4. Use of the Deep Ocean Floor and the Freedom of the High Seas

Besides the questions of who is entitled to exploration and exploitation of the deep ocean floor and how the profits obtained therefrom should be distributed, there exists another problem of a completely different nature. No matter who undertakes exploration or exploitation, these activities should be in conformity with the rules governing the use of the high seas over the deep ocean floor.

A simple analogy between the regime currently applicable to outer space and that pertaining to the use of the deep ocean floor does not seem relevant. Some of the private drafts on the regime of the deep ocean floor have mistakenly introduced into this area of law a number of rules governing the peaceful use of outer space. For instance, the duty to render assistance to any person or vessel in distress, and to inform the proper authorities of any situation or conditions which might constitute a danger to the life or well-being of persons exploring or working in the waters above the deep ocean floor, seem to be concepts borrowed from the Outer Space Treaty.[14] But up to the time of the Treaty there existed no regime generally applicable to outer space, and hence it was the Treaty which introduced many new laws and rules on the subject.

But where exploration and exploitation of the deep ocean floor are concerned, it makes far greater sense that the time-honoured and well-established principles of law relating to the high seas be applied. Identical treatment should be accorded to exploration and exploitation of the continental shelf, on the one hand, and of the areas beyond, namely the deep ocean floor, on the other, in the application of the principles of freedom of the high seas to activities carried on in the superjacent waters of the respective seabed areas. This point is often overlooked. It cannot be too strongly emphasised that the same rules should apply to the superjacent high-seas waters of the deep ocean floor as well as to the waters over the continental shelf. In this respect, Articles 3, 4 and 5 of the Continental Shelf Convention might

---

14. See, especially, Senator Peil's *Proposed Ocean Space Treaty*, arts. 7 and 8.

be brought into play, especially Article 5, paragraph 1, of the Convention:

The exploration of the continental shelf and the exploitation of its natural resources must not result in any unjustifiable interference with navigation, fishing or the conservation of the living resources of the sea, . . .

The questions of who is entitled to conduct exploration and exploitation and which parts of the seabed may be so explored and exploited are quite irrelevant to the application of the principles of freedom of the high seas to these activities. In this regard, reference should be made to a United Nations General Assembly resolution adopted on 21 December 1968 at the 23rd session of the General Assembly concerning prevention and control of pollution and other hazardous and harmful effects which might result from the exploration and exploitation of the deep ocean floor (General Assembly Resolution 2467 B (XXIII)).

Careful attention should also be paid to the matter of liability which may result from exploration and exploitation of the deep ocean floor. The Outer Space Treaty provides for State responsibility, as follows:

Art. 7—State Parties . . . shall bear international responsibility for national activities in outer space . . . whether such activities are carried on by governmental agencies or by non-governmental entities . . .

However, this stricture cannot be applied to ocean operations conducted in connection with exploration or exploitation of the seabed. Both qualitatively and quantitatively, the damage caused by these activities differs from that resulting from activities in outer space. Here again, there is nothing to prevent application of the general rules on freedom of the high seas to activities in high-sea waters. Collisions with equipment or devices used in the exploration or exploitation of the continental shelf or the deep ocean floor, pollution of sea waters or other hazards resulting from such exploration or exploitation, etc., are matters which clearly fall within existing rules of international law.

SUPPLEMENT TO CHAPTER V

1. United States Interests in a Wider Continental Shelf

The United States did not make it clear what its position was on the problem of the outer limit of the continental shelf in the early stages of the discussions in the Seabed Committee over the regime of the deep ocean floor. It simply supported the concept that part of the profits derived from the exploitation of the deep ocean floor beyond the continental shelf should be dedicated to the benefit of the international community. In January 1969, the American Government's Commission on Marine Science, Engineering and Resources, known as the Stratton Commission, whose members were appointed by the President, submitted a report, *Our Nation and the Sea*, to the President and Congress.[1] In this report the 200-metre isobath or 50 miles from the coast, whichever was the greater, was suggested as the limit of the continental shelf. Of particular interest in this Report was the suggestion that there should be an intermediate zone which would encompass the seabed to the 2,500-metre isobath or to a distance of 100 miles from the coast. The 2,500-metre isobath is the average depth of the base of the world's geological continental slopes; the distance of 100 miles is the average width of the continental shelves and slopes. According to this Report, only the coastal nation would be authorized to explore or exploit the mineral resources in the intermediate zone, but in all other respects, the intermediate zone would be governed by the framework recommended for the deep seas. This meant that some of the profits from any production in this area as well, would be used for the international community through the International Fund, while the control of this area would still fall within the competence of the coastal State. It seems that the Commission's recommendations for an intermediate zone embodied a compromise between the view that the control of the coastal State should extend widely enough to include the continental slope and the view that the continental slope should be treated like the area of the deep ocean floor.

There was a great contrast with regard to the issue of the outer limit of the continental shelf between this Report of the Stratton Commission, an advisory body to the President, and the Report of the National Petroleum Council, an advisory body to the Secretary of the Interior, which favoured exclusive jurisdiction over the continental mass seaward to where the submerged portion of that mass meets the abyssal ocean floor (see page 113). Under these circumstances, the United States

---

1. Report of the Commission on Marine Science, Engineering and Resources, January 1969.

124

Government was under strong domestic pressure to take a decision on this issue sooner or later. The State Department, somewhat embarrassed by the Report of the Stratton Commission and seriously concerned that the Report of the National Petroleum Council might encourage unilateral claims of other countries for the extension of their own continental shelves, seemed inclined to limit the outer extent of the continental shelf to the 200-metre isobath. Nevertheless, the United States Government, blamed for adopting a "no policy" approach, was still unable to announce any definite policy on marine affairs. However, what was clear only to the United States was that, whatever might be the way in which the extent of the continental shelf might be decided, or whatever regime might be established for the "area beyond", American enterprises should be able to continue the exploitation of the seabed beyond the 200-metre isobath, and their invested capital should be protected under any future regime.

The United States State Department had come to determine its maritime policy step-by-step in 1970. The report to Congress in February 1970 by President Nixon stated that the United States believed it important to make progress towards establishing an internationally agreed boundary between the continental shelf and the deep ocean floor.[2] But the first step of the United States Government in formulating a policy on the seabed was seen in a statement by President Nixon on 23 May 1970.[3] In it he proposed that all nations should adopt a treaty under which they would renounce all national claims over the natural resources of the seabed beyond the 200-metre isobath and agree to regard these resources as the common heritage of mankind. Thus, the most orthodox criterion of the 200-metre isobath still remained as the suggested limit of the continental shelf. On the other hand, it should also be noted that his statement contained a proposal for an international trusteeship zone for the continental margins beyond the 200-metre isobath. This idea was similar in substance to the concept of an intermediate zone that had already appeared in the Report of the Stratton Commission. In the International Trusteeship zone, as proposed by President Nixon, coastal States were to act as trustees for the international community and would receive a share of the international revenues from the zone and could impose additional taxes if these were deemed desirable. Beyond this area, the agreed international machinery would authorize and regulate the exploration and use of seabed resources. President Nixon's statement represented a very important decision by the United States Government concerning the regime of the deep ocean floor and was one which attracted wide interest in the United States and abroad. While there was no longer much doubt about the regime of the deep ocean floor in general, the United States Government took a step forward toward the determina-

---

2. *US Department of State Bulletin*, Vol. 62, No. 1602 (9 March 1970), pp. 273, 314.
3. *US Department of State Bulletin*, Vol. 62, No. 1616 (15 June 1970) p. 737.

tion of the outer limit of the continental shelf—the extent of the deep ocean floor. The United States was regarded as making a monumental policy decision by finding a compromise in the Report of the Stratton Commission between the Department of Defense which favoured a narrow continental shelf and the Department of the Interior which favoured a wider one. However the fact that the concept of the international trusteeship zone was not quite clear and that its external boundary was not precisely defined would have inevitably caused some confusion in the future, as the lack of precision of the outer limit of the continental shelf in 1958 had led to great confusion.

To implement President Nixon's statement of May 1970 as a concrete proposal, the United States introduced a *Draft United Nations Convention on the International Seabed Area* on 3 August 1970, the first day of the second 1970 session of the Seabed Committee.[4] This was a comprehensive draft of eight chapters with 77 articles and five appendices. The International Seabed Area was defined as "all areas of the seabed and subsoil of the high seas seaward of the 200-metre isobath adjacent to the coast of continents and islands", thus fixing the outer limit of the continental shelf at the line of the 200-metre isobath. On the other hand, the concept of an international trusteeship area was introduced as a part of the International Seabed Area comprising the continental or island margin beyond the continental shelf extending to a depth of 3,000 or 4,000 metres. A part of the profits derived from the exploitation of this area would be set aside for the benefit of the international community. Yet this zone was to be primarily under the national jurisdiction of the coastal State—a situation comparable to the continental shelf.

2. Deliberations on the Extent of the Continental Shelf at United Nations Meetings

The United States draft treaty of 1970 became a subject of discussion among many delegates in the forum of the Seabed Committee only in 1971 after the Seabed Committee was expanded in terms of size and mandate. The United States idea of an international trusteeship zone did not receive broad support among the members of the Seabed Committee. At the United Nations Seabed Committee in the summer of 1970 the United Kingdom and France followed the example of the United States by submitting drafts of their own.[5] However, very few countries at that time were ready to consider these drafts and to start discussions of these concrete regimes for the deep ocean floor. In 1971 some developed nations such as the Soviet Union, Poland and Canada presented their respective drafts.[6] Drafts were likewise submitted by Tanzania and a

---

4. UN Doc. A/AC.138/25.
5. UN Doc. A/AC.138/26, 27.
6. UN Doc. A/AC.138/43, 44, 59.

group of Latin American countries.[7] A draft was also prepared by some land-locked and shelf-locked countries, reflecting their own particular interests.[8] Malta submitted a very comprehensive draft of the ocean regime,[9] and finally, a draft was prepared by Japan after the closure of the 1971 sessions.[10]

Among various proposed criteria (such as depth, distance, a combination of depth and distance, a geomorphological criterion and others), distance or a combination of depth and distance gradually emerged as the most popular. As for distance, a significant number of the developing countries submitted that the 200-mile distance was reasonable and appropriate. In Western Europe, France expressed for the first time in the 1972 spring session its support of the criterion of 200-miles from the coast. In the 1973 session, as a substitute for the conventional term "continental shelf", Japan suggested that the coastal seabed area should be defined only in terms of the distance from the coast.[11] The Soviet Union suggested in 1973 a combination of the 500-metre isobath for depth and 100 miles from the coast for distance.[12] In fact, there were few countries which tried to limit the concept of the continental shelf to the area with a depth of 200 metres. Few denied that a seabed area much deeper than 200 metres would eventually be incorporated by the coastal State, because an element of distance, say 50 or 60, even 200 miles, had been introduced. If the concept of the continental shelf was to be amended in such a way, the sediment close to the continent where petroleum deposits would be likely to be found, would be incorporated by each coastal State under the new definition of the continental shelf.

In the 1973 session the United States submitted a new proposal, *Draft Articles for a Chapter on the Rights and Duties of States in the Coastal Seabed Economic Area*,[13] in order to revise totally the concept of the "international trusteeship area", which, as suggested in its 1970 draft, did not secure wide support in the Seabed Committee. The international trusteeship zone was thus relabelled as a coastal seabed economic area. Although this new draft in its presentation makes a striking contrast with the draft convention of 1970, the aim of both proposals was in fact not so different. In other words, in a coastal seabed economic area, which is seaward of the 200-metre isobath (i.e., the continental shelf) and landward of the lower edge of the continental slope, only the coastal State would have the exclusive right to control its exploitation, while part of the revenue gained from exploiting this area should be allocated to the international community. The real intention of the United States seemed to be to retain an international character for the area beyond the

---

7. UN Doc. A/AC.138/33, 49.
8. UN Doc. A/AC.138/55.
9. UN Doc. A/AC.138/53.
10. UN Doc. A/AC.138/63.
11. UN Doc. A/AC.138/SC.II/L.56.
12. UN Doc. A/AC.138/SC.II/L.26.
13. UN Doc. A/AC.138/SC.II/L.35.

200-metre isobath and to ensure that the right to explore and exploit this seabed area should not be impaired except for a public purpose, on a non-discriminatory basis, and with payment of just compensation.

Land-locked and shelf-locked States, acting in concert in search of a common basis, were gradually linked by strong ties of solidarity and this group took the position that the concept of the broad continental shelf, that is to say the concept of the narrow international seabed area, would render the international regime of the seabed meaningless. Parallel with this, however, by 1973 unchallengeable support had been given to the proposals for a 200-mile economic zone which suggested jurisdiction of the coastal State over the seabed, thus resulting in the amendment of the concept of the continental shelf. Yet, the increasing claims of the coastal States to off-shore seabed areas did not stop at the 200-mile distance as the limit of the economic zone. Some draft articles submitted in 1973 by Colombia, Mexico and Venezuela, by Argentina, by Australia and Norway, and by China respectively, suggested that jurisdiction of the coastal State should extend to the seabed even beyond a distance of 200 miles, where the natural prolongation of its land mass extends beyond this 200-mile distance line.[14] The position in the Seabed Committee at its late stage in 1973 remained unchanged throughout the deliberations of the Third Law of the Sea Conference after 1974. It had become clear that the almost universally adopted concept of the 200-mile economic zone would undoubtedly cover any right to the seabed and its resources within this limit and that any seabed area which could be defined as the natural prolongation of the land territory would be placed under the control and jurisdiction of the coastal States.

3. A New Concept of the Continental Shelf

The Informal Composite Negotiating Text of 1977[15] provided in Article 76 that the continental shelf comprises: (1) the seabed and subsoil of the submarine areas that extend throughout the natural prolongation of its land territiry to the outer edge of the continental margin, and (2) where the outer edge of the continental margin does not extend up to that distance, the seabed area to a distance of 200 miles.

Whatever the fate of the Law of the Sea Conference might be, it is most unlikely that this concept of the continental shelf will undergo any substantial change. Thus, in spite of the geological or geographical features of the seabed, the seabed area up to 200 miles from the coast will certainly be incorporated in the regime of the 200-mile economic zone. The traditional depth criterion of the continental shelf has lost its meaning within 200 miles from the coast. On the other hand, the depth criterion which is interpreted most generously in favour of the

---

14. UN Doc. A/AC.138/SC.II/L.21, L.37, L.36, L.34.
15. UN Doc. A/CONF.62/WP.10 and Add. 1.

coastal State, in other words, the outer edge of the continental margin, which can be 3,000 or 4,000 metres depth of water, is still maintained in the areas beyond 200 miles from the coast as part of the continental shelf.

On the other hand, strong objections from the geographically handicapped nations could certainly not be ignored. Thus, some kind of international character had to be introduced in a regime applicable in the areas beyond the 200-mile zone, in order to soften these objections. The Text suggests as a compromise that certain profits derived from the exploitation by the coastal States of these areas be returned to the international community. It provides in Article 82-1 that "the coastal State shall make payments or contributions in kind in respect of the exploitation of the non-living resources of the continental shelf beyond 200 miles". It is also stated in Article 82-4 that the payments or contributions shall be made through the authority which shall distribute them on the basis of equitable sharing criteria, taking into account the interests and needs of developing countries, particularly the least developed and the land-locked amongst them, and in Article 82-3 that a developing country which is a net importer of a mineral resource produced from its continental shelf is exempt from making such payments or contributions in respect of that mineral resource. Thus, attempts have been made at the Conference to secure the support particularly of the developing land-locked and shelf-locked nations which would otherwise have opposed a wider range of the seabed areas exclusively reserved for the coastal States.

INDEX

African States Regional Seminar on the Law of the Sea (Yaoundé), 34
American Bar Association, 113
Asian-African Legal Consultative Committee, 34

Coastal Jurisdiction,
early claims for fisheries, 3-5
extension, 6-7
over waters superjacent to continental shelf, 99-101
Committee on Marine Sciences, Engineering and Resources, 121, 124
Common Heritage of Mankind, 115-116, 119
Contiguous Zone, 27
Continental Shelf, 77-103, 128-129
adjacency concept, 85, 89
bilateral agreements on, 91, 104
boundaries, 89-98, 104-108
claims, 80-81
customary law, 85
equidistance line, 90-96
equity, 104
exploitability test, 86, 88
exploitation, 98-99, 112-114
installations, 101-103
islands, 96-98, 105-106
median line, 104
outer limit, 85-87, 111-115, 124-128
safety zone, 101-103
sedentary fisheries, 69-72, 74
superjacent waters, 98-103

Dean, 14, 71
Deep Ocean Floor, 77, 109-123
international machinery, 117-119
military use, 111
sharing profits, 119-121
superjacent waters, 122-123

Developing Nations, Interests of, 119

Economic Zone, 34-36
Exclusive Economic Zone,
boundaries, 40, 106-108
concept of, 36-39
land-locked and geographically handicapped nations, 38-39, 40
optimum utilization of fishery resources, 38-39, 39-40
unilateral provisions, 36

Fisheries
abstention principle, 48-49
conservation, 41-46, 61-62, 67
dispute settlement, 63
distribution, 46-60, 64-67
interests and territorial sea, 15-17, 33-36
licences, 59-60
management, 59, 66-67
newcomer States, 54-56
optimum utilization, 38-39
scientific investigations, 41-43
special interests of coastal States, 56-57, 62-63
Fishery Zone, 17-31, 33
evaluation of, 27-31
Geneva Conferences, 17
international agreements on, 22-26
unilateral provisions, 17-23
François, 8, 79
Fur Seals, 53, 65

Geneva Conferences on the Law of the Sea, 8-10, 17, 27-31, 55-57, 70-72, 82-84, 96-97, 112-113
Geographically Disadvantaged States, 38-39, 40, 121
Grotius, 3-4

130

High Seas,
freedom of, 122-123

Informal Composite Negotiating
Text,
continental shelf, 75, 128-129
boundaries, 105-106, 107-108
outer limit, 106-107
exclusive economic zone, 37-40,
66, 106-108
fisheries, 66-67
high seas, 66
marine mammals, 67
migratory species, 66
sedentary fisheries, 75
Institut de Droit International, 6
Intermediate Zone, 121, 124, 126
International Law Association, 6,
113
International Law Commission,
7-8, 13, 54-55, 60, 70, 79, 82,
83, 86-87, 93
International Organizations, Particular,
Committee on Fisheries, 42
Food and Agriculture Organization 42, 59
General Fisheries Council for
the Mediterranean, 42
Indian Ocean Fisheries Commis-
sion, 42
Indo-Pacific Fisheries Council,
42
Inter-American Tropical Tuna
Commission, 42, 46
International Council for the
Exploration of the Sea, 42
International Whaling Commis-
sion, 51
Middle-East Atlantic Commis-
sion, 42-43
World Bank, 121
International Technical Confer-
ence on the Conservation of the
Living Resources of the Sea, 54
Islands, 96-98, 105-106

Johnson, 115

King Crab, 71-74

Land-Locked and Geographically
Disadvantaged States, 36, 38, 39,
40, 129
League of Nations, 5-6

National Petroleum Council, 113,
125
Navigation,
free navigation and territorial
sea, 14
Nixon, 32
North Sea Continental Shelf Cases,
84-85, 94-96

Pardo, 77, 109
Pope Alexander VI, 3

Santiago Declaration, 7
Santo Domingo Declaration, 34
Scientific Research, 41-43
Security,
extent of the territorial sea and,
14-15, 33
Sedentary Fisheries, 69-74, 75
Selden, 3-4
Stevenson, 32
Straits, 32-33

Territorial Sea, 5-17, 32-33
determining factors for the
extent of, 14-17, 32
present law on the extent of,
11-14
United States effort, 16-17,
32-33
Treaties and Conventions
Atlantic Tunas, Conservation of,
45
bilateral agreements on boundaries of the continental shelf,
91, 104
continental shelf, Geneva Convention, 69-72, 74, 75, 79-103,
111, 122-123
revision of, 82
European Fisheries, 24-25, 26

fisheries agreement,
  Australia and Japan, 23
  Japan and Mexico, 23
  Japan and New Zealand, 23
  Japan and Republic of Korea,
    25, 26
  Japan and United States,
    22-23
  Norway and United Kingdom,
    24, 26
fishery and conservation of the
  living resources of the high
  seas, Geneva Convention, 60-
  63, 64, 74
fur seals, 54, 65
Iran-Saudi-Arabia agreement on
  continental shelf, 91
Japan-Republic of Korea agree-
  ment on continental shelf, 104
king crab, agreement on,
  Japan and United States, 73
  Japan and USSR, 73-74

United States and USSR,
  72-73
meshes of fishing nets, 45
Northeast Atlantic Fisheries, 45
North Pacific Fisheries, 48-49,
  64
Northwest Atlantic Fisheries, 45
Northwest Pacific Fisheries,
  49-51, 64-65
territorial seas, Geneva Convention, 8, 27-28
whaling, 51, 65
Truman Proclamation, 43, 79

United Nations,
  deep ocean floor and, 109, 110
  fishery conservation and, 43
  Seabed Committee, 33-36, 104-
    105, 112, 120, 126-128
  Third Conference on the Law of
    the Sea 36-37, 105-106, 128

Whaling, 51, 56